THE SALES BURN-OUT
SURVIVAL GUIDE

The Essential Sales Manual for the Modern World

DAN DRISCOLL

ISBN: 978-1-6847-1191-8 (sc)
ISBN: 978-1-6847-1192-5 (e)

Library of Congress Control Number: 2019916744

Lulu Publishing Services rev. date: 10/18/2019

CONTENTS

ABOUT THE AUTHOR

I welcome you to this book and will share some information about me. I started off just as the majority of people in the world do with a whole lot of nothing and some big dreams. I used to play with Legos as a happy and contented little guy designing and constructing my future empire. And then as if hit by a tornado, my world started to collapse. My parents decided to split up, and that put my dad in a terrible tailspin with his life and finances. After the divorce, he was caught up in a battle with drugs and alcohol for many years, and my mother took over as my primary caregiver. Her goal was to give me every advantage she could. She worked hard to pay for private schools for me and made sure I had everything I needed.

My mom's only advice to me was not to follow her career path—accountancy. She hated her job and did it only to take care of me. I always appreciated her hard work and the sacrifices she made to take care of me; that example gave me a sense of responsibility and drove me to make something out of my life. I challenged myself to rise up and produce someone my mom could be proud of.

When I was little, my goal was to own a business and enjoy that, which drove me to become the most curious kid on the planet. Whenever I met someone who owned a business, I'd ask every question under the sun in regard to how to be successful in business. Go figure—everyone said I had to learn how to sell. So guess what I did?

My passion has always been business but with a focus on sales, which in my opinion determines success or failure in business. I got my first start in sales selling cars at age fifteen at my uncle's and dad's car lot. To say I was a natural at it would have been a giant stretch, but I outworked everyone else to save face.

At that point, sales became my life, but it wasn't the enjoyable life I had dreamed of. It appeared to be filled with anxiety and pressure. Then one day, I invested in a sales book by Zig Ziglar and everything changed. I got so much value out of that book that I must have read every sales book out there. I have been studying sales systematically for the last twenty years, and what I have learned has allowed me to not only sell but also to enjoy it.

My goal in writing this book was to give others the information they needed to enjoy selling as a career but not just to make more money because—trust me—that alone isn't the answer to a life of happiness. I'm not a professional writer by any means, but I wrote this book to share what I have learned, not wow you with my writing skills. Not to brag, but I have made myself a millionaire several times over using the information in this book.

When I took my first real sales job out of college selling Yellow Pages ads in 2010, I made $250k my first year using the information in this book. It was amazing when I had my accountant mom prepare my tax return and see the progress I had made. Her eyes lit up when she realized I had developed the skill of earning enough money to support me for the rest of my life, an amazing gift.

I want to give the same gift to your parents and family. The skills you will learn will allow you to protect your family with the certainty that no matter what happens, you'll be bringing home a paycheck and more important teach you how to enjoy your career again.

And don't be shy. I include here my LinkedIn account, so please reach out to me or come to one of my events if this book makes a difference in your life; I would love to hear about it. This has become my life's work, and your feedback and kind words motivate me to keep making a difference and helping other professionals take back control of their sales careers again. Now let's turn to the introduction and start our journey together.

https://www.linkedin.com/in/dan-d-driscoll/

INTRODUCTION

Has selling changed in the last twenty years? The last ten years? Five years? Two years? The last year? Yes! Sales is constantly evolving, and that's been especially true over the last few years.

The massive growth of social media has been the main catalyst for these changes. I want to teach you ways to let these changes help your income. Many sales reps have seen social media and the internet ruin their businesses. I used to sell Yellow Pages ads, and to say the internet wiped my job out is an understatement, but social media and the internet are not something to be afraid of; they are actually the greatest opportunity of the decade. They are making many sales pros seven-figure incomes, which was unheard of just a few years ago.

But the rewards are only part of the reason you should master the art of sales. Think about the consequences if you don't. So many people never invest the time in educating themselves, and where do they end up? I feel they choose to be ignorant because they fail to understand the consequences of ignorance.

If you master the concepts in this book, you will learn how to sell hundreds of people at once. For example, you will learn how to do webinars and use the attendees to sell each other. You will learn how to leverage one happy client who purchased what you're selling to get other attendees to buy. Your first purchaser will start the domino effect. How powerful would that be—having your clients sell your product for you? I'll show multiple ways to do that in addition to the webinar. Interested? Trust me; that's just the tip of the iceberg.

I wrote this book specifically to prepare you for the changes occurring with this digital shift and more important, to prevent you from being left behind. The biggest threat to your income in this shift is being an unskilled sales rep. So many jobs are going to be eliminated by automation or artificial intelligence, and sales is one of those jobs that will soon be drastically affected. We'll always need to buy things, but the process of buying will change, and if you're not prepared to change, you could very easily be eliminated from the workforce.

This book is designed to show you how a few simple, learnable skills will protect your income when these shifts occur. It will also show you how you can transform your career by gaining the skills you need to start a business or lead a team of sales reps. Success in business comes down to selling your product or service and knowing how to manage the people in your organization.

This book will give you what you ask of it. I suggest you ask a lot, reread it often, and highlight it wherever you want. Every time I reread it, I take away more, and I wrote it! I suggest reading the entire book or at least your highlighted notes once a month to keep the ideas fresh while you implement them.

I have broken this book into three easily digestible parts. The first is about selling in the new social era, the second is about selling yourself, and the third is about sales management though I didn't write that part just for sales managers. Trust me; that section is well worth reading. It's a very informative part for anyone in sales, and it will show you how to manage yourself.

Today, the average reader doesn't finish more than the first chapter of a book, but don't allow this book to become one of those. I designed it so you can read it from start to finish or jump right into the sections you feel are most relevant to you. I know that after you take in and apply this content, you'll read and reread every section and reference them often.

This is the manual for sales in our new era, but a manual is only good if its information is retained and applied. It is essential that you read this book and perform the activities in it while expecting this book to give you the knowledge you need to achieve the income and lifestyle you desire.

Too many people have weak goals and weak ambitions. I know that by your taking the time to read and master this book, you're above average. You want more and are willing to put time into learning the skills to make your dreams a reality. Play full out while you read; have a pen and notebook handy. Pretend you're studying for the biggest test of your life because you are.

And last, enjoy this book. I spent a lot of time writing it away from my family, friends, and career, and I did it for you. All I ask in return is a simple favor—when you finish it, message me your feedback and how this book has helped you; that would mean a lot to me. I want you to set a goal for yourself of reading this whole book; I want to be here to hold you accountable. Are you with me? Are you committed to finishing this book?

I look forward to connecting with you online and hopefully getting to meet you on a webinar or a seminar one day.

Connect with me on LinkedIn at https://www.linkedin.com/in/dan-d-driscoll/. If you message me, I'll send you some special bonus content.

Go on and do it now—I promise it'll be worth it.

Thanks for connecting. Let's begin…

FYI: 55 percent of those making their living in sales admit they don't have the right skills to be successful.

FYI: Trained sales reps make 50 percent more than untrained sales reps do!

Why Social Media Is Something You Really Need to Know

So what is social media? I know we understand the meaning from an application sense, but I need you to understand social media from a sales and business perspective. Social media is a platform for a person to get quick attention. Social media will allow a person to quickly get the attention of the entire world with as little as one post. If something is popular and liked on social media, it can quickly get more exposure than the president of the United States does.

I've seen YouTube videos of cats at play getting hundreds of millions of views and at the same time getting millions of dollars' worth of free exposure. These videos in the majority of instances were also filmed on a cellular phone camera in someone's house, no professional studio—crazy, right? I mean, you can touch millions of people with something we all have in our pockets. Just pull your phone out and hit record and you could be talking directly to millions in countries with names you don't even know how to pronounce.

Social media for a salesperson is simply a tool to build credibility while capturing attention. Social media will open communication doors that are often closed through traditional media. If I wanted to sell the CEO of Amazon on our marketing company, I could attempt to use email to break through, but what are the odds I'd get his attention? If I used social media and asked for a friend request, I might get through—slim chance but maybe. If I really wanted to get through, I'd design a viral post that tagged Jeff Bezos, Amazon's CEO, and get a few million views. Doing something creative like that would definitely get his attention, and when used properly, it could be instrumental in delivering the experience that gets an appointment and helps close the sale.

In this book, I'll show you how to get attention like that, how to get huge clients, and more important, how to master social selling.

When I was a selling Yellow Pages ads after college in 2005, the only tool I had to contact clients was the phone, and getting someone to answer my call was hard. I would often call someone five even ten times before I could connect on the phone with him or her. Now, with social media, you can get hold of your clients 24/7 with a simple tweet or post.

Social media can also simplify maintaining relationships with your clients by allowing you to connect with all your clients on LinkedIn to share relevant info about your service. You can effectively touch your entire client base hundreds of times per year with by posting something a few times a week. If you posted one time on LinkedIn and had all your clients as friends, they would see your message every day. You could also get reminders of clients' birthdays from Facebook and with one click wish them a happy birthday. These simple strategies alone will help you form stronger relationships with your clients.

In the next chapters, I will break down very simply how I would sell using social media in combination with the traditional forces you already know and use. The way I'll combine old and new styles will for the majority be eye opening and for others will be a refresher in some ideas and strategies they have likely been underutilizing. Either way, I promise this will be the best sales book you have read.

Remember that repetition is the key to mastery, so read and highlight any part of this book that you know works but are not using. Knowing something is far different from applying it, so let this book force you to apply the concepts you know will advance your career. Often, one well-executed idea is all it takes to change the trajectory of your career. Let this book provide you with that one idea and the power to bring that idea to fruition.

I've devoted my life to finding what works and applying it constantly. This book is about taking what I have mastered about social media and simplifying it into a process that you can use every day to quickly increase your income while working fewer hours if you choose. Social media and the internet are the leverage to grow your earnings and reduce the hours you work.

If you want to have this book make a difference in your life, and I know you do, follow my instructions. Let me coach you on this journey to grow your sales skills; follow along and write the answers to the questions in the book. The more active you are, the more this content will stick in your brain and increase the value you provide your clients. What you don't know does hurt you in sales. Let's get committed to sharpening the saw.

If you are going to take the time to learn, why not spend a few extra minutes to make sure you retain it? Imagine I'm in the room with you going over this content; don't read passively. By answering the questions and interacting with me, you'll be driving the content deep into your mind. The more you do that, the more likely you'll be to remember it, use it, and have it make a difference in the quality of your life.

Let's begin by answering four questions. Get a pen and write in your book to start this journey.

Why is being top performing sales rep important to you?

What are your biggest accomplishments so far?

Why do you want to master sales?

What's at stake if you don't succeed at sales?

Tell me and I forget, teach me and I may remember, involve me and I learn. —Benjamin Franklin

PART 1

Sales 101

This book is about more than just social selling. It will cover everything you need to know to either run a Fortune 500 sales organization or make a seven-figure income as a sales pro.

The biggest problem with sales professionals nowadays is the $100k trap. Ten years ago, making $100,000 was like the holy grail of sales jobs. Now, if you're making $100k, you are very likely struggling with car payments and private school tuition. Crazy, right? That's now turning into a poverty standard.

The salesperson of 2019 needs to set his or her sights higher than $100k. And more important, higher than anyone has ever earned in his or her current position. We can't let the superstars in our current organization be the limits on our success.

This book will unlock tools that will make higher income easier and more probable for you, but again, knowledge without application is a waste. My goal is to create time for you by making you more efficient while increasing opportunities for you to present your product or service to prospective clients. The ultimate limit on your success is the number of presentations you make, and this book will show you how to maximize that number.

In this first part, I address how you can use social media to get in the door with large and small companies, design a video presentation that closes business for you, and run a webinar to generate leads 24/7. I will also explain how to use your CRM, your customer relations management process, and not get used by it, how to use templates to save time with emails, how to get hired for your dream job, and so much more.

Sales Basics

So what are the sales basics nowadays anyway? I mean, everyone seems to hate salespeople. Did I just say that? Yet everyone is selling nowadays from the multilevel marketers to little Suzie's Girl Scout cookies. With social media, it seems everyone is peddling something online 24/7. Your role in the present sales world is to become an expert with real knowledge you can deliver to prospects and find ways to increase their ability and solve problems they face.

With the current deluge of information flooding our brains, people have become terrified of missing something or more important looking like idiots. Just the other day, I did a webinar, and hundreds of people signed up, but many missed it. We had more than 500 sign up, but only 177 showed up. A good number of those who missed it were emailing me to see if they could somehow view a recording; they were terrified of missing out. They didn't want their competitors to have intel they had missed. But I know the real question you have is, "How did he get more than 500 people to sign up for his webinar?"

The answer is that when you sell in today's environment, how you perform your presentation is far less important than how you look online. You can be the greatest salesperson in the world, but if you have a few bad reviews on RipoffReport.com, you're finished. The internet can propel you to greatness or bury you with one post. The reputation and the branding of a sales rep were unheard-of concepts just a few years ago. When I purchased a new car recently, the sales rep wanted to get a pic of me in the car for his Instagram account. Do you think this picture is for anything other than to get future business?

The internet allows your entire sales career to be posted online to serve as a reference for your success as a sales pro. Countless photos of happy clients will actually help the sales rep and more important the dealership attract new clients. As this sales rep markets his personal brand, the car's brand, and the dealership's brand to thousands of connections hundreds of times throughout the year, he will be setting himself up for great future months, quarters, and years.

At a hockey game one time, a guy behind me had a fishing tackle company. He had grown his business to $30 million in sales on social media alone. Each time his company sold a product, it would post a pic and tag the purchaser on its Facebook timeline. When the purchaser was tagged, it would go to all of that person's friends and family. That boomed his tackle business with essentially no marketing costs; it added only seconds to each transaction to create the Facebook post.

The other thing this action did was allow the business to friend all the business's clients making it super easy to continue to market new products to his client base every time he posted. How many more referrals could you get if each of your clients was tagged with a picture after he or she purchased something from you?

Social websites are starting to make emails obsolete. I view my emails as work and do not want any promotion in my email inbox. On social media, however, I'm looking to kill some time, so I'm okay with relevant promotion there. I also pay attention now and have become friends with the people I'm doing business with. People do not cancel relationships. Social media is a way for you to truly friend your client base. How powerful would it be to connect with all your clients on social media?

Now onto social media and selling. But before you turn the page, answer a couple of questions while your mind is thinking. Let's use this new knowledge to generate extra sales for you. Please get your pen. If you are going to invest in yourself, why not spend the extra seconds to make it worthwhile? Application of the knowledge in this book is the first step to creating the compelling future you desire.

What are three benefits to using social media for sales in the context of your career?

How can you use social media to increase your sales?

How can you develop a strategy to friend all your clients?

How can you capture happy clients' pics or stories and post them on social media?

1.1 Social Media and Selling

Key Statistics

1. Visual content is forty times more likely to be shared than words! Invest in getting some infographics or visuals to promote yourself and what you're selling.
2. Video ads are taking over on LinkedIn. A total of 55 percent of marketers were using video ads on LinkedIn in 2018.
3. On LinkedIn, try to post tips and lists of five.
4. A startling 80 percent of B2B leads come from LinkedIn versus 13 percent on Twitter and 7 percent on Facebook.

> By 2020, 85% of the buyer-seller interaction will happen online through social media and video.
> —Josiane Feigon

This chapter will redefine selling. It will be about placing ads on social media and about using what's free to increase your sales. Before I let you in on this secret, I'll tell a quick story about when I was selling Yellow Pages ads and literally going out and distributing business cards on every table known to humankind in a feeble attempt to get new business. I did that for years. How many calls do you think I got from doing that? I can't remember one deal I closed as a result of dropping a card off someplace. That was because no one wants to call a salesperson for a sale. People are terrified of salespeople even if they need something. Ever wonder why so many sales reps have titles that do not say "sales"?

The interesting thing is when I ask reps to spend five to fifteen minutes a day working social media, they say they don't have time, but they'll spend hours putting cards out everywhere they go. It's so much easier to just message a business on social media every time you stop in instead of dropping off a business card. The other thing is that when you drop off a business card, it usually goes right into the trash can. If, however, you talk about the owner on social media and tag him in a post, what are the odds you'll get noticed?

In the past, I had put out a post with a special deal a boat dealer client of mine had on his front lot when we did a visit. Doing this post was simple; all I did was take a picture of the boat that had a screaming deal sticker on it and posted it to social media with a tag to the business owner. One of my contacts actually called in and purchased the boat, and I got noticed for linking the two.

Businesses notice when you engage with them on social media. You don't have to get a sale; just the act gets you attention. Just liking a few of their posts before your sales appointment can make a big difference in your conversion rate as well. Social media is where friends interact. You want to be your clients' friend.

Social media is an excellent way to gain access to direct contacts or the true decision makers in an organization. Social media does not have a lot of spam filters on it right now, especially LinkedIn, for business sales. You can literally message anyone you want with a premium account. I have connected with some Fortune 10 companies from a contact plan on social media by sending one InMail on LinkedIn for instance.

Social is such a great way to open the door for a sales presentation, and believe me, it's so underused. For example, if I solicit someone at a car dealership, I can find his or her Facebook and learn all about him or her and set myself apart from the competition by connecting with him or her. People still value relationships. Today, the strongest relationships seem to be online and not face to face for the majority of people.

So how do you get a connection with your clients on social? I have asked during a conversation, "Are you on Facebook? Yes? Let me connect with you. I want to show you my car collection or my fishing pictures." Then you can message them on Facebook something they're excited about. Every time they get an alert, it gives them a fun notification; people love seeing these alerts on social sites.

Social sites have even been accused of setting up a system like a casino; the notifications are said to release endorphins every time someone gets an alert. This excitement around social friend request and messages helps brand both you and your product as exciting.

I will be going very deep into social throughout this book. I know you now are starting to see the value, right? The main purpose of social meets my first quote.

> The more ways you have to connect to a prospect the
> faster the deal will close.
>
> —Dan Driscoll

Social media combined with traditional marketing can take the needed five to eight contacts to close a deal and get the deal done on the first visit. If I friend you on Facebook and use that to develop a relationship, I can often close the deal on the first call. Think about how many sales reps connect with clients on Facebook. Think about how this will set you apart from your competition.

I can also do a ton of follow-up just by messaging on Facebook in a nonsalesy way and actually get a response from a client. Use all the social websites and find the one the client uses the most. I for example use only LinkedIn, but the majority of the planet right now uses Facebook.

How can you ask clients for their social media accounts? What is the angle or reason they would want to friend you?

How can you improve using social media in your current sales routine?

1.2 The Right Sales Process

If you can't describe what you are doing as a process,
you don't know what you're doing.

—W. Edwards Deming

There are many sales processes out there, and almost all talk about building rapport. I think that's the worst and most dangerous word when it comes to sales. Sales at its core is about getting the buyers' attention and trust. If buyers believe you have something of value, they will buy it in most cases no matter how little rapport they have with you. Many times, I'll run away from a salesperson who is trying to build rapport with me especially if in an insincere way. I will in many cases simply buy the product online so I can bypass the communication and time wasting that comes from artificial rapport building.

People are dying for connection, but they're getting that online, definitely not through salespeople. A good connection is necessary to allow the conversation to progress. The conversation however should not be centered around rapport; it should progress naturally.

The key part of opening a call is getting the buyers' attention and quickly establishing a hook that will show them that your product or service could be extremely valuable to them. Start the process with a strong hook so they'll listen to your entire presentation. Once prospects start listening, provide enough value that they enjoy and continue listening to the entire sales presentation. In this new era of selling, I replaced the word *rapport* with this: sales is the ability to demonstrate empathy for your client while displaying your sincere love of your solution or product.

When you align your passion and love for your solution with your clients, rapport will develop naturally. Asking the right questions to find out if your solution is really best for clients forms the foundation of rapport. Your questions will show your sincerity and build rapport naturally and automatically. Rapport today counts only if it's natural and comes across as genuine care for the prospect. Consumers are too sophisticated to fall for fake rapport, so ask questions that show you care. Your job is to find out how you can provide tremendous value to your clients, not sell your clients. When sales is done properly, clients will never think of buying anywhere else.

What questions can you ask your clients to show you care about them?

What questions can you ask to truly find out what their problems are?

Step 1: Paying Attention

> "No matter how nice the house is on the inside no one will see if there is a dead body in the front yard."
> Dan Driscoll

Getting attention—good attention—is the most important piece of the sales process. If you're bad at getting attention, you'll get very few sales no matter how good of a closer you are. When a sales rep comes to me with a missed quota, the first thing I do is troubleshoot the attention phase of the call. Normally, the rep is not opening the call in a way that prompts the buyer to listen. In many cases during the open, the buyer is half-checked out on a poorly opened call and is simply waiting to exit it.

Many sales reps think that their prospects are listening and thinking about making the purchase. The level of engagement you get with prospects when you open calls is key to whether they will truly consider buying your product or service. I like to even ask this question at the start of my presentation: "Do I have your full attention?" Their answer gets them to tell me where I stand from the start.

You get attention by making a giant claim, one that makes them want to listen. Just having rapport with prospects will not get them to really listen as much as a big fat claim would. When we're selling our service to federal contractors, I'll say, "Would it be worth five minutes of your time if I could show you how to protect your business from the next recession? Our average client does $197,000 in additional revenue their first year, can I have five minutes to quickly show you our solution?"

That claim normally gets their attention. You want it to sound almost too good to be true but worth listening to. I normally like to circle back and ask, "If this solution worked half as good as we went over, would it still be a good value for you?" By using a big fat claim to get prospects' full attention, you'll increase the number of presentations you can make and also the likelihood that the buyers are listening to the presentation. Have you ever watched a trailer and knew you had to see the movie? That's what a big fat claim does for your presentation. Many studios spend more money on the trailer than they do on the movie. Sound strange? They know that if the trailer is no good, no one will watch the movie.

What is a big fat claim you can make to get the prospect to want to listen to your presentation?

Step 2: Permission

> Nobody can hurt me without my permission.
> —Mahatma Gandhi

And Gandhi also meant to say, no one can sell me either without my permission.

My mother always told me to ask for permission. I do that on every sales call not just to please my mother but also because it helps close sales. We will talk more about the questions you want to ask on a sales call later, but trust me—without the prospects' cooperation, you won't get honest answers to questions or even client interaction in most cases. You'll also risk being grouped into the category of pushy salespeople. Drill this question into your brain: "May I have your permission to ask you a few questions?" You'll want to ask it during every sales call.

It's better to ask forgiveness than ask permission if you know the answer is no, but you'll need to get permission—verbal or nonverbal—before you present your product or service. By using this simple technique, you'll always get it. The key is learning how and when to ask for permission so you don't get turned down. When you ask for permission, your goal should be to get a 100 percent yes rate. Gaining permission to probe is key to getting your prospect to follow through on the discovery phase of the sales process. Having your prospect answer some questions is the only way you can build the value you need to get the sale to close.

I like to ask for permission right after I gain commitment to do the presentation. That puts clients in a yes mood and will make sure they let me ask some probing questions. Again, asking, "Can I have your permission to ask you a few questions about your business/needs?" will open the door for a zero-objection discovery process, so burn that question into your brain. Forgetting to ask for permission to ask questions will make prospects ask themselves, *Why's he asking me these questions?* They'll say, "I'm busy. I have to go. Email me something."

Ask for permission before you ask any questions, and make sure you ask right after they agreed to give you their time for your presentation. Sales reps are often classified as rude and pushy, so you want to quickly establish yourself as not the typical sales rep. Show clients you care about their time and business in the long term.

Step 3: Questions

> The question is the answer.
> —Thomas Vato, Questology

Thomas forgot to add, "Ask the right questions and the sale is done!"

There are three types of questions: hot-button questions, fire questions, and closing questions. I call them these for many reasons but mainly because every time I mention the word *close*, people jump out of their seats and listen.

The closing questions will be the part of this process I want you to take away the most; hence the name. You don't need to use all these questions in any order, but if you can do the first and second in order and go to the closing questions only if you're ready to close, I recommend that.

For complicated products, you'll uncover and address a lot of problems and will likely go back and forth with many questions. I don't like to get buyers ready to close multiple times but then take them back to the discovery phase, so stay with the hot-button and fire questions and then when ready lean on the closing questions as the gas to get the deal closed. Use a lot of questions when you close; that should be the longest part of your sales presentation.

Hot-Button Questions

Every question you ask should have a specific goal—getting the prospect to recognize the value in what you're selling. Many salespeople try to first figure out if the prospect has any money and simply ask prospects for their revenue numbers; that's a huge mistake; that will make them feel like a piece of meat and will often prevent the reps from giving them a full presentation no matter how much money they have. And many clients inflate their revenue numbers anyway.

At a business conference I attended, the speaker asked everyone who had done over $10 million in business to stand. When everyone did, I knew they were lying; only 6 out of 100,000 businesses do more than $10 million in sales. A professional can tell if prospects have money by a lot of implicit ways. I find that asking questions to gain clarity on how serious they are about the purchase is actually more important than the money anyway. How many super-rich but super-cheap people do you know? How many do you know who bought something they couldn't afford just because they had to have it? I'd rather take someone in love with a product whoever that is.

Your number one goal when asking hot-button questions is to ask as few as possible. Always try to discover the clients' revenue and years in business online without asking since that data is publicly available in most cases. If you ask clients for their addresses, you can plug that into Google Street View and get a pretty good picture of their financial qualifications. I have also never found a hot-button answer by asking for a business owner's income for instance. I don't think I would start to ask for the order by saying, "Because your income is $125,000, I feel you should buy our most expensive solution."

Here are some hot-button questions for businesses and consumers.

1. Why did you call in/take my call? What sparked your interest?
2. Just from your initial observations, what aspect of my product do you see as most valuable to you?
3. Just so I understand your business, can you give me a quick explanation of what you do?
4. I'm always curious. If you don't mind, can you tell me why you started the business?
5. If you had a magic genie right now that could solve one problem with your business, what would it be?
6. If everything went perfectly in your business in the next five years, what would it look like?
7. If you were to do business with a firm like mine, what would be important for you?

The key with hot-button questions is to make sure you don't ask anything that will make business owners feel you're hunting for their wallets; that will kill the deal no matter how great your product or presentation is. They will curl up and protect themselves from being sold as soon as they are spooked. Prospects in the fetal position will no longer give quality answers to your questions, and you'll lose all ability to find any new angles and ways to create value for the client.

The key with the hot-button questions is to find out issues the customer has that your product or service can solve. People buy things that solve problems, and they spend more on bigger problems. Use the hot-button questions to allow the clients to talk and then turn into Columbo and find out all the clients' problems.

What are a few hot-button questions you could create for your sales presentation?

Fire Questions

These are questions that expand the size of the problem. They're essential for getting your client to act. Fire questions normally aren't fun to ask, but without them, the sale will often be stuck in the buyer's thinking zone. If I uncover a problem you have had for years, what is the chance that uncovering the problem alone will force you to act to solve the problem? The answer is very slim; you may listen to me, but taking action will be another story. You've known about your problem for years but have never solved it. Uncovering the problem is not the fuel for action; you have to fan the fire to get it to take off. And hot-button questions are that fan. Hot-button questions should frame the consequences for inaction. Your prospect is much more likely to act to avoid pain than gain pleasure.

Whenever people tell me they have back pain, I always tell them my girlfriend is a chiropractor and exchange numbers, but they almost never make an appointment. They had been living with back pain, but that wasn't enough to get them to act or they would have already acted. They choose to deal with the pain and are not really looking for a solution at this point. When a prospect is in the initial stage of a sales process or thinking phase, fire questions are the propellant that moves the problem from something that would be nice to solve to an urgent, must-solve problem.

In the purchase paradigm by author Chet Holmes, 3 percent of the population are buying now, 6 to 7 percent are open to buying, 30 percent aren't thinking about it, 30 percent think they don't need it and 30 percent know they don't need it. So when you ask questions, you allow prospects to move from the thinking about it and or not thinking about it phases, which is the majority of leads are in, to the buying now phase which is essential to close the sale. Often, sales reps think prospects are leads only if they are in the buying-now phase, but the best prospects are those who move from not thinking about it straight to the sold phase; that's because they aren't shopping around for price in most cases.

The better you get at asking these questions, the quicker you will move a browser into the sold column for a quick, high-margin sale. Think about the times you saw things that you just had to have. Did you normally get the product at the lowest price? Think about product you were in the buying phase for months. How much better deals did you get on those products? Would you rather be the salesperson who gets a quick sale or the one who does the work of ten sales reps dealing with a price shopper?

Fire questions are powerful because they will make your prospect want to look for a solution with urgency, which is essential to close a sale. Most salespeople never ask fire questions; they just probe till they find a problem and try to go for the close. Buyers will then say they need more time since they aren't ready to solve the problem. Uncovering a problem is not the goal; it's only the first step to reaching it—the sale. If you only uncover the problem, the sale will be stalled until another salesperson asks fire questions or the problem naturally grows on its own. Have you ever had prospects tell you, "Call me next quarter"? They're saying that their problems aren't big deals at the time, that you should call down the road when they'll set aside time to deal with it.

When I was selling Yellow Pages ads for Verizon, I would always follow up on leads that had been pitched by other reps who did not close the sales and ask them fire questions to get them over the edge. I'd be called names like thief and snake, but the truth was that those prospects would never have purchased without the fire questions. The previous sales reps hadn't asked the questions to get the prospect to create their own urgency. The previous reps were waiting for these clients to create their own urgency, and in today's world of endless distractions, that doesn't occur often. Urgency is the only reason a sale closes, and increasing the size of the problem creates tremendous urgency for action.

A fire question should ignite prospects and get them to want to take immediate action. A good fire question will make the problem feel unbearable and turn it into something that needs to be solved immediately. To sell my girlfriend's chiropractic services, when someone tells me he or she is in pain, I go right into a fire question, not a close and definitely not just handing out a business card; we all know how to find chiropractors.

Here are the fire questions I ask for my girlfriend's chiropractic business.

- Where does it hurt?
- Does it feel like bone on bone yet?
- Is the pain affecting your sleep?
- Is it effecting your production at work, yet?

- So you did nothing all weekend. What is backing up at home because of this pain?
- Could you live with this pain another couple of weeks or do you really want to fix it now?

My asking these fire questions normally makes someone more open to scheduling a free consultation. The biggest fire question is the bone-on-bone one; with it, I'm asking, "Do you want to get it fixed before it's too late? You have a limited window to fix the problem and return your body back to full health, and you want to make sure you don't miss that window."

While your mind is turning and the ideas are churning, let's take some action. What are some fire questions you could ask to flame your prospects' problems and get them to want to act now?

Closing Questions

If you use the hot-button and fire questions correctly, you may feel you don't need to ask any closing questions, which you ask to make sure the deal is closed. Often in sales presentations, reps don't create enough excitement to close the sale and avoid the day-after sales anxiety that clients experience. When I think of closed deals, I think of clients that are so happy about their purchase, that they want to sign for five years of business and refer five friends to me right then. A closed customer is not just someone who has seen enough to sign; a closed customer is someone who has seen enough to refer me to others and become a lifelong client. If you always think about getting someone that sold, you'll never have to chase around prospects and hope to meet your quota; you'll know that your clients and referral base are strong.

So many salespeople try to close too soon and end up with no close. This no-close phenomenon is normal, so don't feel bad; we've all gotten trapped in it at one point or another. But let's make a commitment to use these tools to make sure our prospects are so sold that they're ready to refer us business at the time they sign the contract.

Closing questions are the ammo to land bigger deals and higher close ratios on your presentations. The true key to your sales presentation is to remove a lot of the fluff and spend the main chunk of your time in the question phase; buyers should be very interactive during well-done sales presentations.

Closing question get buyers to tell you the exact benefits they see from your solution. I can tell you from doing this for many years that you never know what the buyer likes until you ask; top closers always ask. When I used to sell cars, my dad told me, "There's an ass for every seat. You just have to ask the right questions."

Here are some types of closing questions.

- If you were to book an appointment for my girlfriend's chiropractic business, what would have been the reason you did it?
- If you did not have this pain, what would you change in your day-to-day life?
- How much more sleep do you think you would get if you didn't have this pain?

Here are some closing questions I used when I sold Yellow Pages ads.

- If you were to change your headline of your ad to feature emergency work, how do you think that might impact the results of the ad?
- If we were to move your ad size up to give you more exposure, what would be the biggest reason you would have to make that change?
- If you were to give me a referral, what would have been the reason you did that?

Step 4: Recommendation Phase

Keep this phase short; the recommendation should be already handled mostly by the questions you have asked. Many sales reps feel a need for a long, drawn-out presentation. The longer your presentation or recommendation phase is, the more salesy your product looks and the less likely it is to close the sale. Your presentation should be so simple that your prospects understand every aspect of it.

Asking prospects if they have questions and understand the solution is superior to any flashy visuals. This is the part of the sales process in which buyers are actually getting nervous and the sales reps need to slow down to prevent from running them over. Many sales reps actually get nervous and speed up during the close; make sure you intentionally slow down during this process and project your calm, confident energy to the prospect.

For instance, I will normally go right into the recommendation phase at the end of my closing question. I'll then do a quick problem recap and close: "Based on your desired outcome of _____, this is what you need to do, and it's $4,995. I can get this started for you today. Is that fair enough?"

When you ask for an order with confidence and certainty after a asking the right questions, 50 percent of the population will say, "Let's go," and the other 50 percent will ask for more information since you gave very little. You then ask, "Do you want the big picture or the details?" They will answer, and then you'll have permission to give your product pitch. You always want to get the clients' permission to do product pitches; otherwise, you risk sounding salesy. The key in this phase is to ask for the money with certainty and expect 50 percent to give you the money no matter what on the first request. The others might take five or eight times, but you'll close them all with persistence.

Be persistent, and be certain when closing. In the recommendation phase, buyers want to know you're certain they should choose your recommendation. When you present, you want to make the buyers feel that there's not another program they should even consider. The buyer should be saying, "This is a no-brainer." You'll likely be asked for discounts during this part of the sales process, but make sure you hold firm. In 90 percent of the cases, buyers will ask for a better deal but really only want to hear, "This is the best deal we can do for you."

Step 5: Ongoing Closing

Closing should be occurring during the entire call. I know everyone knows the ABCs of sales—Always Be Closing. This rule is true, but most people get confused by its real meaning. Some buyers need to be asked for the order more than eight times to move over the fence from the maybe zone, and the maybe zone is a huge problem. In my sales process, I always try to keep back a nugget I can drop on my prospects' scales to push them over the edge if they get stuck in the maybe zone too long. I purchased a vacation tour I had been kicking around for a few months because the company sent me an email offering me a free hotel upgrade if I acted now. When I purchased a new mattress, the salesmen gave me a few free pillows. He could have offered them at the beginning of the sales process, but he wanted to see if he needed that cherry to move me over the fence in case I stalled. I got extra value since I didn't know they were included with the sale. That was a win-win.

What could you hold back or use as a cherry in your sales process to close deals?

The human brain is risk adverse; we need to be certain we're making the correct move, and that's why we need salespeople. The fire questions will give the prospect additional juice to get off the fence and close the deal. I like to bring up again the fire questions if I run into an issue at the closing table. In my experience, when prospects are reminded of their giant, urgent, must-solve problems, they often quickly move ahead with the sale. The goal is to keep calm and know that prospects need to consider the pain they'll experience by not buying. When prospects are stuck, remind them of the potential hell of not buying and the potential heaven of buying.

Fire Questions

"If we let this problem grow for the next five years, what will be the consequences? Can you really afford not to handle this now while it's still solvable?"

Getting prospects to feel the pain of not using your solution will move them more than the benefit of using it at this stage will. You want the prospect to be scared of missing out by not closing now.

Think of the news; what are the headlines you read? You want to make sure your prospects are looking at the giant problems that need to be solved, not the potential problems they may encounter with paying for your product or service.

At this phase, you should be prepared to ask for the order multiple times to get the deal. Don't forget with existing clients to still follow this same rule; everyone needs to be asked to close multiple times. Many sales reps treat their renewal clients different from new prospects, but that's a mistake. It can often take a better strategy to renew a client than to sell a new one. You have to make sure you're not thinking your renewal clients are laydowns. Have a strong plan of attack and game plan for your existing clients; they are your most valuable asset in sales.

Existing clients need to be convinced every year to buy, so keeping good notes about the pain points that made them buy in the first place will really help you close the deal in year two and beyond. No renewal client just renews; they all need to be resold. As a successful sales rep, you're in this for the long term. You should always be asking yourself, *How can I get referrals out of this client and make it easier to renew the business next year by keeping excellent notes in my CRM?*

To summarize closing the deal: have your set closing program and plan to try to close up to eight times before giving up. All deals are closed between the first and the last call; the question is, who's going to make that last call? When I sold Yellow Pages ads, I was often the tenth caller on a lead but ended up getting the business. I was skilled at what I did, but timing and luck will beat skill any day.

Fair enough is what I call another close; I learned it from Eric, my business partner. "Fair enough" may be the most popular phrase in closing. I use it combined with "Let's move forward" as my dominant close. I'll repeat this a lot because it's that important.

The reasons fair enough works so well is the isolation of the deal and the use of the yes principle. When you get clients to focus on a fair deal, that gets their minds off the perfect deal they had been looking for. Deals that get done are fair for both parties. Your goal as a sales rep is to get the prospect to want to make a fair deal with you. Buyers buy only when they're willing to make a fair deal.

1.3 The Sales Funnel

In sales, money doesn't just fall out of the sky. There's a set system buyers follow before they purchase. This system is very simple but is often not understood even by top sales reps. So many of them are obsessed with getting signed contracts that they often forget the components and pieces that are required to assemble a signed contract.

Understanding these pieces provides the foundation for increasing the number of signed contracts you receive. You'll also learn to manage the sales funnel as a sales manager in the part on sales management; it contains invaluable information especially if you're not a sales manager. I'll exceed your expectations in that section, but let's get back to the sales funnel.

With the sales funnel, the parts equal the whole. If you don't understand the parts, you won't even begin to put together a six-figure sales income.

I've made a simple Excel document with the numbers and formulas for the parts of a signed contract. Message me on LinkedIn and I'll gladly send it to you. Now's the time. If you haven't already connected with me, do so at https://www.linkedin.com/in/dan-d-driscoll/. This tracker will let you adjust the numbers and learn how you can affect your income with each part. Here's a sample of one I put together for a client.

Ratios

Dials/leads	100%
Contacts/dials	40%
Conversations/contacts	60%
Appointments/conversations	70%
Appointment shows/appointments	80%
Proposals/appointments shows	80%
Closes/proposals	50%
Average revenue per client	$1,200

Leads	1,500
Dials	1,500
Contacts	600
Conversations	360
Appointments	252
Appointments kept	201.6
Presentations	161.28
Proposals submitted	50
Closes	25
Revenue	30,000

This list seems like common sense, right? Yes, it is common sense to know the steps, but what do they mean? And more important, how can you use this intel to help you sell more? I address in depth how to apply all this to help advance your sales career in the management part. In this part, I'll show what each piece means, the falloff points where you lose sales, and how to master the parts to a sale.

The first item on the list is leads. The more you have, the more chances to sell you have, but that's only if you call them. What's interesting is the difference in your production when you call all your leads twice or even three times. How much could that add to your sales commissions? It takes on average three times to get a contact to answer the phone, so if you're calling them just once, what are your chances of catching them?

And what kind of voicemail message do you leave? Do you send an email after every phone call? I want to try to get as many contacts out of the way as I can at the beginning of the sales cycle.

When you call your leads will also have a huge impact on your contact rate. I vary the times I call my prospects. If one doesn't answer at eleven, I'll call again at four or perhaps at seven thirty in the morning; I want to know when they're most likely to answer my call. Never assume any time is a bad time to call a prospect unless the prospect tells you that. HubSpot puts it this way.

When you think about the structure of a typical office day, you realize at 11:00 a.m., most people are wrapping up tasks before taking lunch. Similarly, at 4:00 p.m., they're winding down for the day.

They're likely hesitant to start a new task, which makes it the perfect time to take a phone call from you.

I called all my leads one time and got a 40 percent contact rate. If I called those who didn't answer the first time again, I might get a contact rate that was 50 percent higher. If I got hold of 50 percent more leads, that would change the math and give me 50 percent more income, an additional $15,000. The more changes you can make at the top of this formula, the more dollars will come out on the bottom line. Look at it this way: if you don't call your leads, how will you ever get appointments with them? If you never send out a proposal, how would clients ever buy from you?

I like to show this model to get sales reps to realize it's not all about closing, which plays a part of course but closing is also the hardest part of the model to influence. We can for instance increase our percentage of clients who show for sales appointments by sending them appointment reminders. If we maintain our same closing percentage, that will on its own increase our revenue.

Another key point is how many contacts turn into conversations. Having a big hook helps make sure we get prospects to want to listen to our presentations. The more engaging we are during our initial phone call, the more likely we are to get prospects to stay tuned till the end of our sales presentations. This is a key fallout point in the process. You can't close a contact who doesn't have a meaningful conversation with you.

The next key fallout point is going from the conversation to the appointment. Many times, this is put off for many days. The more time between the conversation and the appointment, the lower the odds are that the prospect will actually show up for the appointment. Another key item that affects appointment shows is how the appointment is framed. Tell prospects that you'll block off an hour of your time for them, and also tell them that if they have to cancel to please call you so you don't waste your time. Doing so will give you a much bigger chance of getting prospects to show up for appointments.

Reminders are also a great way to increase your appointment appearance rate. You can text reminders and send calendar invites for example to remind prospects of the appointments. I often text prospects a few minutes before the call to remind them I'm calling. Business owners typically react to things all day, so you often have to pin them down in advance with multiple reminders to make sure they don't miss your appointment.

What's the best system to increase your appointment show ratio? I can tell you it's none of the above. It's simply not to schedule appointments. Often, prospects use the appointment as a stall technique because they see no value in your product. Asking the simple question, "What do you want me to focus our appointment on?" will give you a chance to continue asking questions and in many cases get the prospect to allow you to present your solution on the first call and skip the appointment altogether.

Our number one goal is to sell a prospect on the first call if possible. If we can find the real problem on the first call, we'll have a great chance to continue to the presentation on that call. Buyers have time for things worth their time and attention. Your job is to make sure you're worth their time and attention. Asking questions and using fire questions to make the problem more urgent will fast-track the clients' timetables to solve their problems and get them to advance the timeline and want to take your call.

How many appointments amount to presentations? I mean, how often are we demonstrating our solutions? Just because clients show for appointments doesn't mean we delivered a presentation. A presentation would signify that we have presented our entire solution. Making our presentations fun and exciting is often the best way to ensure that a big percentage of our prospects listen to our entire presentation. Having a lot of interaction and customization of a presentation will also help ensure a high degree of interest in the presentation. If my prospect is engaged in my presentation and I use his needs to customize it, I'll have a much better chance of getting his full attention during a call.

Interaction makes presentations easy. By asking questions, you let clients handle the bulk of the load of the presentation. The client should be talking 80 percent of the presentation, and questions are the fuel for the sales process. If you take away one thing from this book, take away the power of questions.

The next piece is how many presentations lead to proposals. If I presented my product, the client may or may not be interested in it, so proposals will be sent to clients that were receptive to my presentation. Your goal should be to send a proposal to every client who is receptive because clients can't buy without proposals.

Next is the close rate on those proposals. Closes are very rarely the reason buyers purchase. When the entire sales process is well performed, the close should come naturally. Buyers should be asking you, "How do we get started?"

When you're closing, the key is to ask with the expectance that you'll get the deal because your solution is the only option for your prospect. Keep asking until the client accepts your proposal, but be prepared for that to not happen on your first request. With the sales funnel, the most important thing is to understand how all these pieces work together. Without appointments, even the best closer will be without sales.

What does your sales process look like?

What are the key milestones your prospects move past before they purchase?

What are the points in your process that have leaks you need to patch?

What can you do to fix those leaks?

1.4 The Four Questions Buyers Ask before Making Decisions

All decisions are made when a buyer answers four simple questions. These questions are almost always unspoken, but they are essential to closing a sale. These four questions are so simple that you'll likely say, "Duh!" when you hear them. But they're not answered on almost every deal that doesn't close. The real goal on a sales call is to think about how you can get buyers to answer these four questions as quickly as possible. And the word *rapport* is not included in any of them. Is rapport really required nowadays? It is only if it's sincere.

Take notes and pay attention as we look at these questions as if they were the lifeblood of your sales career. They are.

Question 1. "Is this solution real for me?"

This question has absolutely nothing to do with whether the solution is a good solution; it's if the solution is real for the buyer. So many buyers will say that something is great but just not for them, a really nice but expensive car or suit for instance. So many sales reps will hear buyers say how great a product is but fail to understand it will solve a problem for them. That happened to me when I was selling a technology program to work with the federal government. Many prospects would tell me how cool everything was but not buy because they didn't understand how it could help them or viewed it as too complicated for them.

That prompted me to allow them to actually experience the product in a customized demonstration. I would ask the clients what kind of work was most profitable for their businesses and actually pull up some available federal work and ask if it would be profitable for them. The sale closes when buyers say your product is really cool and this is for them. Make sure you get them to imagine using the service.

Realtors will ask clients if a particular room is big enough for their furniture; that prompts the clients to imagine moving into the place. Get your client to imagine using your service and check off the first question, "Is this solution real for me?" Answer the following questions; consider this spring training in sales.

How can you get your prospects to know your solution is what they want and not just some cookie-cutter solution you pitch everyone?

How can you get their buy-in that your product aligns with their identity?

Question 2. "Can I use it?"

The critical question "Can I use it?" is often not answered in sales presentations. Everything has so much technology in it nowadays. Even my Vitamix blender came with a CD. Practically everything also needs to be registered online. A lot of things may look simple to the salesperson, but the client has a different point of view, and it's often an unspoken objection you have to uncover.

Let the client test drive your solution if possible to answer this question. I like to employ a lot of testimonials in particular from those with very little ability using the service. Colleges include minorities in their advertising to let everyone know they can succeed in college. They're not speaking just to minorities; they're trying to portray people who look normal but are of a lower social standing than the typical college person. These ads are targeting a particular audience—those who think they weren't cut out for college.

When I sold fireworks, I mentioned that my grandmother liked to shoot off the mortars with her grandkids to let the parents know their kids would be safe. I'd even show them a picture. That allowed me to sell the more expensive fireworks even to single mothers.

How can you show your prospect they can really use your service?

Question 3. "Will I use this?"

That question applies to some extent to every purchase. If you sell a product that requires clients to really go after something like MLM or a training program that takes a lot of time, this might be a big question and an often essential but unspoken objection. The older the prospect is, the higher the tendency is for this question to come up. This question might be your biggest stumbling block since they purchased an item similar to yours in the past and not used it—a weight-loss program for instance. Once the client admits that he or she can and will use the product, your deal is basically done.

The best way to get the client to answer the "Will I use this?" question is to talk to the prospect about how other clients already use the solution. Showing the prospect multiple relevant and applicable ways to use your product will affirm in your prospects' minds that they will use the solution. You want them to visually see themselves using the product.

Think about the last time you were really excited about buying and using something. I had a giant TV eyed out several years ago and imagined my friends and I gathered around it eating hot wings and watching the big game. How can you get your clients to visualize using your product? How can you get them to associate the feelings they want to feel with your product? How can you show the client that using your product reinforces their identity?

When I sold our technology program at US Federal Contractor Registration (USFCR), I would talk about how it sends emails out every day to let you know when opportunities come available so you can pick and choose the ones you want. Many clients find this makes it so easy for them use consistently since they're always checking their emails anyway. This feature makes sure they never miss perfect opportunities.

Get your clients to imagine using your solution more than once. You could talk about how a set of golf clubs would be great for practice after work as well as at the annual tournament. By doing that, you just got the client imagining using the clubs twice in one sentence.

How can you get your clients to imagine using your solution multiple times?

Question 4. "Is the exchange better than the alternatives?"

When your buyers ask, "Is the exchange better than the alternatives?" they are often comparing your product to something else. Our technology solution to working with the federal government could cost as much as a new vehicle; buyers were thinking, *Do I want a new truck or this technology solution?* To answer that, you have to understand what you're up against. By asking, "If you were shopping and had (mention the cost of your highest priced product) to spend in the next twenty-four hours, what would you buy?" When I ask this question, I can kind of get an idea what else is on their radar.

To answer this question, you must first talk about why your product is a good deal to buy now in comparison to the alternatives. You could say a new truck is always $35k while this program is $50k, but by buying it now, they can get a discount. You could also tell the prospect that this program will pay for the truck with the profits it generates in the first year.

I want to make sure buyers see how much better my product is than the others while creating a reason to buy it today. Your buyers are on the fence because they don't see a reason to buy your product right now, so you have to supply that reason.

What are the four questions that a buyers asks before they purchase? Write them again to burn them deep in your brain.

Out of the four questions, which question do you think is most impactful in your current sales presentations?

How can you get your client to answer the four questions quickly in your sales process?

1.5 What a Lead Wants

Make a customer, not a sale.
— Katherine Barchetti

This part will allow you to put yourself in your prospects' or customers' shoes and let their needs become yours.

What does a lead really want? Think about when you are just starting a purchase process; do you really want a salesperson? The answer in most cases is no, but do you *need* a salesperson? That's the real question. If you are nonthreatening at the start of the process, you can build the excitement needed to get the client ready for a salesperson.

A lot of salespeople will say, "That buyer is just a looker, a time-waster." What unsuccessful salespeople fail to realize is that all buyers start by seeking information; they all start as lookers before becoming buyers. The prospect wants to find information in a nonthreatening or obligatory way especially at the start of their information search. As a salesperson, your main goal is to get buyers to see that you align with their interests in this initial phase. They need you to know they aren't ready to buy today and will determine if they can trust you today. Aligning your needs with theirs will bridge the trust gap.

You know that prospects are not ready to buy what you're selling until they see they can't live without it. Your job is to show them they can't live without it. Clients want to buy things; they don't want to just be sold things. They will become buyers when that one thing comes across as irresistible. Your job as a salesperson is to know how to move them from lookers to buyers. That process starts with understanding how to work with the looker.

Here's what you should do to increase your lead conversion.

- Understand that lookers are not ready to buy yet.
- Give them the information they need quickly with no expectations of a quick sale.
- Show that you are more interested in helping them than selling them something.

Once you accomplish those three things, you can easily open the lead and move to the next part in the sales process. So many low-percentage sales closers fail to understand the importance of pulling the lead into the funnel. These reps are easy to spot; they will often complain about leads being the wrong types or just lookers. A good salesperson understands that buyers who feel pressured from the start will say anything to get away from the salesperson and even lie about not being interested. If someone showed up at your car lot and said he or she wasn't interested in buying a car, would you believe that?

List several examples of when you told a sales rep you weren't going to buy but were really ready to buy.

List several times you lied to a sales rep to avoid a high-pressure presentation even when you did need information.

1.6 How to Handle a Lead

Leads are either the greatest thing in the world or they represent work. If you've been cold-calling, you might be screaming in joy to get a lead. Some sales reps are blessed to be in lead-rich organizations while others are stuck in impoverished, leadless organizations, but one way or the other, leads are only as good as you make them.

You may have never had to cold-call or have been blessed with an abundance of leads and not be excited to see leads, which you might consider a chore. But when you get leads, remember that they're just looking for information. In many cases, they might have filled out a contact form for any number of reasons. Most likely, the lead form was filled out for reasons other than to talk with a sales rep, so don't be alarmed if a prospect isn't jumping up and down when you call.

Identifying and relating to leads is the first step to handling them. You need to put yourself in the lead's shoes and ask yourself how you'd want to be handled if you had taken the steps the prospect had taken leading up to asking for information. If the lead came from an online source, you need to respond fast before the lead goes back online elsewhere; this is because 78 percent of customers buy from the first responder. Calling a lead within five minutes of getting the lead increases conversion rates by up to 900 percent. Don't worry about calling the lead too soon; the quicker you call, the less competition you will have working your lead. Speed also yields a nine times hirer conversion rate.

When I landed in New Zealand one time, all the car rental places were closed. I filled out three leads forms that night and the next day got three calls. Of course I bought from the first caller. Was he the best salesperson? Hard to tell; I listened to only one proposal.

When I call a lead, the first thing I do is recap how I got his or her information. I then quickly dive into a hot-button question to start the call rolling forward. As I mentioned, just because people fill out online forms doesn't mean they guarantee to talk with a sales rep. Please don't get mad at prospects for wasting your time or affecting your close ratio just because they won't talk with you because that's simply normal. Sales reps have to earn the right for prospects to take their calls. A lead is not a reservation for a sales appointment; it's simply a reason to knock on a prospect's door.

Your open of the lead is ten times more important than anything else. If you have a great open that works with cold calls, try opening your leads the same way. I spend time learning about their business and reference their websites. I also like to have set questions to go over with them before I call.

Make sure you don't open a call in salesy way; start off with a recap of how you got their information. I like to say something like, "Your information was just put on my desk. I'm calling to give you some information on a new Volkswagen. Do you have a question about inventory, or did you just start looking? Would you like a brochure or a no-obligation test drive?" You could also ask, "What specific information can I get to you about our technology solution?"

These are just a few simple ones that I use to get the lead open and moving down the sales process. The better you get at lead opens, the quicker you'll realize that there are no bad leads. You will notice that the types of leads you used to throw away will start being added to your close ratio and client list. The key is to learn how to treat leads in a nonthreatening manner so they will trust that you have their best interests at heart. It's framing the conversation to provide value first, and that is normally free information.

How can you open your lead to get the best return?

How soon should you call a lead to get the best conversion rate?

1.7 The Job of the Buyer and Seller

> When a woman is talking to you, listen to what she says with her eyes.
>
> —Victor Hugo

There are two types of communication—verbal and nonverbal—and in sales, you need to master the nonverbal variety. This lesson is your silver bullet to sales success, so pay attention. I learned this amazing nugget when I was a fifteen-year-old working at my dad's and uncle's car lot. My uncle used to say, "All buyers are liars"; that was one of the first sales lessons I received. Buyers will say and do whatever it takes to look uninterested in what you are selling because they're terrified of being sold.

When I was selling cars, buyers would often say a price was too high for a car in this or that condition and then make a lowball offer. I learned to pick up on their body language. If someone kept looking at a car as we were talking, I knew he really wanted the car and was just acting. Uninterested buyers just left. Those who kept talking were most likely on the hook and just looking for confirmation that they were getting the best deal. Prospects want to hear that you're giving them the best deal to satisfy their egos in that regard.

Many salespeople think that buyers' objections are real when in reality they're just automatic responses—"We're not buying anything today." "Is that your best price?" "That's out of the budget." All these responses are just things all buyers say habitually. It's the buyers' job to make these comments and express these concerns; sellers need to understand that these are baseless objections and actually mean the buyers are interested.

It is not the buyers' job to help close the sale; it's their job to stop any sale from occurring and to buy what's best for them. Make sure you're aligning your mission with theirs to help buyers get what they want; that turns an uphill battle into a smooth downhill coast.

I could write a whole book on this concept, but here's a quick way to remember this, a concept that is hard to understand only if you fight it: buyers will always state the negatives, so sellers will always need to refocus them on the benefits and the solution. Sellers have to be certain that the benefits outweigh the negatives to get the deal closed. Sellers don't have to remove all the negatives; it's actually to the sellers' advantage to acknowledge the buyers' issues and agree they're real. Agreeing that the product has faults will let buyers stop pointing them out and allow sellers to point out the positives. As soon as you agree with prospects, their gardens of objections wilt overnight.

When sellers are really good at their jobs, they'll make the benefits seem so great that negatives are no longer in the picture. When I'm at the produce stand by my house and complaining about the fruit not being as nice as that in our organic food store, I'm not going to the organic food place; I'm there buying fruit at the local, run-down produce store. The merchant should simply state, "Yes, I know this fruit isn't of the same quality as that at the organic store, but its lower price should more than offset any blemishes."

What are some of the fake negative things buyers say in your industry?

What are some ways you can get buyers to refocus on the positives after they make negative observations?

How can you stay calm in the sales process when the buyer objects? Can you take a deep breath? Can you squeeze your fist? What can you do to keep your energy and state up?

Remember that when buyers are giving feedback, they are normally very close to closing. Stay calm and don't give up because victory is near.

1.8 Agreement Frames

Agreement frames are the most important part in dealing with sales objections and closing the deal that I know. They align prospects and sales reps, and they're the only way I know to properly handle objections.

If your blood pressure boils during the close, read this chapter daily till you can't disagree with anyone ever again. Seriously, it'll be worth that much to you. Being able to agree with a prospect is a skill that allows deals to close. Agreement violates a natural human response—to stick with your current thinking no matter what—so it needs to be conditioned, but the results are worth it.

The more you get used to agreement frames, the more likely you are to be a positive and likeable person. I have three agreement frames taped to my computer monitor: "I agree." "I understand." "I'm with you." These are just some of the many I have used over the years including, "You're right." "Done." "That's correct." "I respect that." "I appreciate that." Write these down every morning before you start selling because they're that important. When you're in a close and you agree with a prospect, you'll be shocked at how easily the sale closes. If you argue with prospects at any point in the buying cycle, the majority of them won't buy. Arguments do not lead to sales; agreement frames are the water that extinguishes the fire of objections.

Agreement frames work so well because people love to be right and making them right disarms them. Once you disarm a prospect, you can come to a conclusion of your negotiation. When criminals have bombs, the police always disarm the person before they start getting the hostages out. You have to get prospects to put down their weapons—their objections—and come back to the reason they listened to your sales presentation in the first place, stop looking for more objections, and look again at how your solution solves their problems.

Have you ever had prospects who no matter what your solution was kept raising more objections as if that were their mission? Our brains are designed to protect us and thus will find fault with everything that resembles a change. Sales is not about eliminating what's wrong with the solution; it's about making buying more attractive than not buying. Get your prospects to go beyond their objections so they can focus on the solution you offer.

Using an agreement frame is not deceptive or a violation of your ethics even if you don't agree totally with prospects. The agreement frame is simply agreeing with prospects' thinking based on where they are at in the sales process. A good example of this is when a buyer comes in and says, "I'm just looking," or "We're not buying till next quarter." A salesperson who asks, "Why not right away?" will put buyers on the defensive. If the salesperson says, "I understand. Do you mind if I still show you our solution so you can have the information you need when the time's right?" he or she will have disarmed the prospect and the sale can move forward.

"You're right" is the most powerful agreement frame. Try using that response in an argument in a relationship and watch what happens. Everyone is right in his or her mind. Salespeople have to acknowledge their clients' opinions before presenting their own. Both parties think their opinions are better, you do not want to argue but show them another way of thinking. Your prospect can be right and still buy. But they will not buy if you make a point to prove them wrong in most cases.

What are six agreement frames?

What happens when you fail to use one?

Why is an agreement frame correct and not a lie or deception?

1.9 Objections

Objections are commonly hated and even feared by some salespeople. Some sales reps are so worried about objections that they don't even ask for the order for fear of getting a no. Objections are the language of the buyer; those who don't object are most likely not buying. Ever had a presentation that looked perfect? Buyer said yes to everything but the contract never comes in? In most cases, if you don't get objections out, you won't close.

Not all objections are hard objections; most are actually soft objections—those that aren't true or simply automatic responses. Buyers have been conditioned to object; we've all been told, "Don't get sold" Pro salespeople understand that they are in control of situations and that objections are a normal part of a sale. If a prospect is not objecting, you have either not pitched a high enough dollar amount or you're working a corpse that's too scared to tell you how he or she feels.

Objections are part of buyers' language and mind-set; it's self-protection. Salespeople who are not hearing objections should ask questions to uncover them. Ask, "What are some potential issues you might have if you went forward with this solution?" Don't be afraid to ask the hard questions; prospects already have, but they're just keeping the answers inside. Get those objections out so you can move the sale forward.

All objections—all real objections anyway—are normally not spoken. Real objections are often embarrassing and thus not voiced in my experience. I may say that a beautiful girl is not my type, but the real reason I don't ask her out is that I'm scared she'll say no.

Think about times when you gave a sales rep a baseless and automatic objection. When I was in the process of buying a truck, the sales rep asked me if I was ready to buy, and I quickly responded that no, not until I visited a few more dealerships. The truth was that I had been to three dealerships and I had just told my girlfriend that we were buying at that place. The sales rep said that no one could beat his deal and that I needed to buy now. I left the dealership and ended up paying more for a truck that was not exactly what I had wanted. Ego is a powerful thing in sales negotiations; always let the prospects win or they'll take their business elsewhere. I hadn't wanted to feel pressured; I wanted to be in control of the process, so I gave the salesperson a fake objection. So often in sales, reps just need to get out of the way and let buyers close themselves. Buyers who are shopping want to buy, so let them buy.

When you get a soft objection, acknowledge it and move on; don't make a big deal of it. Just smile and continue to close. I used to sell high-end cars, and almost every buyer said they were too expensive. I'd simply smile, look them in the eyes, and say, "Wait till your friends see it. They'll all want a ride." The objection wasn't real; my buyers drove for miles to look at cars they knew the price of. Don't battle soft objections; if you do, buyers will defend their objections and in most cases go somewhere else.

I liked to challenge rather than attack soft objections. I'd ask, "Is that your only objection?" Most people came up with a few more, but I'd ask, "Why don't we just drive it and see how she feels?" Pro salespeople realize most objections are fake; they smile and move the call forward rather than attack them. Buyers object; that's their natural role as buyers and means they're about to buy something, so be thankful for them. All they want is for you to agree with them and move on to the close.

Here are the questions I ask when I get objections.

- On a scale of one to ten, where are you with the product/ service?
- What would make it a ten?
- I get that all the time, and I understand your point. Doesn't the value of the product outweigh it though?
- Is that your only objection?

Reading this book is good, but answering the following questions will drive the content deep and make a true difference in your sales career.

What are the soft objections you get?

What are the hard objections you get?

How can you keep your blood pressure down when a prospect object?

Did you answer the questions? Please get a pen and do them ... and thank you for those that already did them, you are already on your way. This is powerful stuff, right?

1.10 Closes

Salespeople love closes and will often buy books on sales just to read what they say about closing and learn some closes. Closes are necessary in sales, but they're often overused and misunderstood. If for example you fail to get clients to experience your product or service, no close on the planet will work. Businesspeople and especially those with sales experience can detect flashy closes, and those types of closes may ruin more deals than they create. You still should know a ton of closes even if you don't use them all. Be sure to have many weapons when you go to battle just in case. However, you'll use only one at a time, and you should sharpen and use your best close first; consider the others as backups.

The best closes are commands, not questions. If you're using a take-it-or-leave it close, you just made a lot of money by reading and applying the contents of this chapter. One of the worst closes I have ever heard was that of a rep who worked for me; he'd say, "The bus is at the station. Are you going to get on or let it pass you by?" First of all, it gave options, which is horrible. And more specifically it gave an option that allowed the like client to keep things the same and spend no money. Do you think that was a hard decision to make, to not buy the car with that close. Second, who wants to ride a bus? Make sure to use empowering metaphors if you use them at all. A prospect might want to take an Uber instead.

I'm going to give you five closes you should memorize, but I warn you not to use all five on the same prospects if you want to close. Make sure you understand the first parts of the sales process. Simply reading these closes won't work. You need to practice them out loud and role-play them many times. Make sure they sound crisp, and repeat them at least five times out loud to make sure that you have them down cold and that they're not rusty right when you need them the most. You should master each of these closes by practicing them for, say, seven days each before moving on to the next.

When you need a close, you won't have time to think, so make sure these closes have become automatic. If you fail to memorize the closes, you will use the naturally conditioned close, most likely, "Do you want to do it? Yes or no?" That's not anywhere near as effective as the closes below. Having a million-dollar presentation and a ten-cent close is a shame. Spend the time to master and role-play these closes.

Here are my favorite closes in order of importance.

1. Let's move forward, fair enough?
2. If you know you're going to buy sooner or later, why not have the benefits now? Let's get started. Fair enough?
3. This is the right product for you. We both know it. Sign here.
4. I'm not going to let you miss this opportunity. Sign here.
5. Think about how much of difference doing this now will make for you. Let's move forward. Fair enough?

Answer these questions.

How can I make sure my closes don't sound salesy?

How many times should I practice my closes?

1.11 The Fair-Enough Close

"Fair enough"—those may be the most important couple of words in sales. I use these every day when I'm selling. Asking if something is fair enough has had a huge impact on my sales close rate. Using these two words will increase your closing ratio and remove many objections simply because it points the prospects to consider if this is or isn't a fair deal. Fair enough works so well in closing because it points to a fair deal. And remember from earlier fair deals close and that they are the only deals that work in the long term. Buyers always want the best deal possible. How many consumers will spend hundreds of dollars on gas and lost time to save a few dollars on items at Walmart?

The fair-enough close helps redirect buyers from focusing on getting a hot deal or the best deal to getting a fair deal; that's when a deal has the potential to close. Fair deals provide the win-win necessary to keep the economy going and more important keep your prospects closing. All buyers understand that they can't take all the profit out of the deal, but they'll often still try to do that unless the seller gets them to look at the value, not just the price. Focus clients on answering the questions "Will buying this solution provide more value than its cost?" and "Is this deal fair for me?"

Have you ever spend so much time looking for the best deal, gotten worn out, and ended up never purchasing anything? You simply gave up on the process. The perfect deal can never be found. Buyers will buy once they get it in their heads that your solution will meet their needs and is a deal fair for them and better than the alternatives. You need to get them to that point.

Fair enough can be used multiple times during the call, not just during the close. I will use it to open a call: "I'm going to get started now and should be done in fifteen minutes. Is that fair enough?" In the open, I ask, "Fair enough to get your permission to give you my presentation?" You can also use fair enough when the client asks you a question you want to answer later: "I'll get to that at the end, fair enough?" Remember, fair enough is actually a command that gets buyers thinking about a fair deal rather than the best deal. Fair deals are the only long-term deals that close. You might offer a teaser to get a client into your firm, but at some point, both sides need fair deals to sustain their relationship.

In today's online world, many buyers are so obsessed with saving money that they forget how much their time is worth. Those who go for the cheapest price often end up buying something that doesn't really meet their needs. Hasn't that happened to you?

Good sellers make buyers feel they're getting something much more than the best price—they're getting a great value and the best solution for their problems. Buyers want to buy, and fair enough allows them to focus on getting a fair deal they can find quickly so they can get back to their other important matters. Remember to use and practice the fair-enough close daily. It's the most powerful close I know.

Why is fair enough so powerful?

When can you use fair enough?

1.12 Webinars

I'll get into some ways to make money in the new digital world we live in. Depending on circumstances, some sellers may not be able to take advantage of all these tactics, but I've made each section short so you can read each one anyway. At some point, you may work somewhere else where they let you these tools, or you may be able to persuade your current boss to let you experiment with these tools.

In the next five years, selling will change a lot; will you be prepared for it? Read this with an open mind and get ready to find a way to truly leverage your time and sales.

Webinars are one of the best new ways to sell. I know what you're saying: "I can't do webinars in my current sales job" or "I'm not a webinar guy." I'm with you, but let me tell you that might be the reason you need to do them. In marketing, doing what your competition fails to do gives you all the advantage. Plus, how can you tell it won't work if you or your competitors have never tried it?

You need a reason for clients to attend a webinar. You also need an offer that allows them to take advantage of it. If you sold cars, you could email all the clients who came in for the month about your webinar on how to get the best deal on a new car. It could include the best time to buy a car, the best deals on your lot, and how warranty purchases can really help make their savings higher. This would be a way to reengage your prospects for the month with one email about a thirty-minute presentation. Clients typically stay for an entire webinar and actually listen and take notes as opposed to those who sit through a typical sales presentation without listening or taking notes. Webinars are effective because they offer a nonthreatening way for a prospect to interact with a salesperson; they deliver info without obligation and pressure.

As your email list grows, you could easily end up with a few hundred potential clients listening to each webinar. Think of the value that branding yourself for thirty minutes up to an hour with each client would provide you. This is just one example, but with social media, webinars are exploding. I think sales will end up almost exclusively being done on webinars in the future. How many times have you ever had to pitch a good number of people at once?

The skills you will gain in this section will make an impact on your other presentations as well, your face-to-face pitches. The three core concepts we will focus on in this section will be getting your prospects' attention, providing them value, and giving them amazing offers.

Webinars allow presenters to pitch products or services to hundreds of people at once, and they can establish the knowledge and credibility of the presenter. The benefit of social media is that prospects can purchase or interact on the webinar and create a possible mad rush for an offer. You could offer a signed book to the first five people who buy the offer and say thank you every time someone buys a book live from the webinar. This live interaction could get your attendees to race to be one of the first five buyers.

Using webinars to present information is a low-pressure, no-obligation sales tactic. Very few people would sign up to be sold something, but they will sign up to learn something in a passive, safe, and nonthreatening manner. What could you offer your prospects to get on the webinar? What information could you give them? The three most important things to know before they buy their first house? How to negotiate the best deal on your new car purchase?

The real key to webinars is to get the prospect to join the live webinar and not watch the recording. Prospects who watch rebroadcasts never watch it as intensely or as attentively as those who watch it live do. You want prospects to feel that they're in the room with you, and being live does that.

Your biggest asset in a webinar is the ability to get your audience's full attention during the webinar. If you can keep prospects on a webinar for an hour, your chances of closing them are very high. Think about the last time you spent an hour with a sales rep and didn't buy something. Been a while, right? That's why webinars are so effective.

Here are the keys to a good webinar

- Have an amazing hook—a reason for them to listen.
- Explain at the beginning how the webinar is structured and set up with the best to come at the end such as a surprise or great offer they won't want to miss.
- Drop great content—nuggets—every three to seven minutes.

- Be real and authentic, not too polished. Think a reality TV show.
- Have lot of visuals.
- Have a webinar-only offer.

The first thing I want to do with a webinar is make sure I get the audience's total buy-in. This is a very key but an often missed step. When you fail to get the audience's total buy-in, you will notice people exiting the webinar very quickly shortly after you start. To get the audiences' buy-in, I try to figure out who is on the webinar, figure out what they want to see, and find a way to get them to say yes out loud or internally that this webinar is for them.

You want clients to feel that you're speaking to them and that they're supposed to be on this webinar. I like to poll them to find out what types of clients are on the webinar and what they're interested in. Having clients see a box to check that looks specially designed for them will satisfy the first part of the webinar.

The last webinar I did was on the four paths to success as a federal contractor. The first thing I did was figure out who was on the webinar. I cheated and asked people first when they signed up to fill out a survey that was very helpful. I had four types of people.

1. New business owners (25 percent)
2. Established business owners (10 percent)
3. People who wanted to start businesses (40 percent)
4. Employees of businesses (25 percent)

I also asked them what they were looking to take away from the webinar.

- to learn the basics of federal contracting (registration)
- how to get their first contracts (bidding)
- how to get more-profitable contracts

With that data, I structured my presentation to get buy-in, but I also got the attendees to feel they were in the right place by having a box to check that fit their criteria. How could you make your prospects even if not on a webinar feel they're in the right place? Car dealers will ask, "Do you have a specific car in mind, or are you just browsing today?" to get customers to feel comfortable about whatever stage they are at in the car-buying process and feel confident about talking with the sales rep.

This is how I opened my webinar.

Hi, I'm Dan Driscoll—author, amazing federal coach, and consultant. Today on this webinar, I'll show you the four paths to success in federal contracting:

Before I get started, I want to say hello to everyone on the call and say you're in for a real treat today. Please close your browser and give me your full attention for the next thirty minutes. This will be the best webinar you have ever been on about succeeding in the federal marketplace. This content alone is worth thousands of dollars, and by being fully present, you'll get that value.

So on this call, we have four segments of viewers. We have a bunch of successful business owners who are looking to expand, and we have new businesses that want to find a way to take their business to the next level. I also have some federalpreneurs (clients looking to start a business solely to take advantage of the federal market), and some employees of successful firms that are using this as a training ground.

This presentation will cover a lot of basic and advanced concepts from registration to bidding to scaling your business. On this webinar, I will align and connect each piece to show you how to form a winning federal contracting strategy for your business. Some of the content may sound similar to things you've heard before, but I promise that each piece has some unique differences. This content is not available outside our paid wall for future viewing. Pay attention, take notes, and use this information to add another stream of income to your business.

Webinar Structure

A webinar should be set up to have an open that brings everyone together on the call. Once the webinar is open, it should drop a few nuggets to make sure the audience is excited and sees value in committing their attention. Once speakers have the audience's attention, they should present themselves as real human beings, not superheroes, and tell their stories that showcase how they came from nothing and with the right training rose up. Nothing does not mean just poor; it means showing how learning the content in the webinar is something anyone can learn and apply. Good speakers can paint pictures of the mistakes they made before they learned the content and how it changed their situations.

Only at that point should the content be delivered. Speakers will identity and magnify the problems the audience has and make them fire questions that are self-answered and prompt immediate action to solve the problems.

What happens if you don't buy a new car before that big road trip and get stranded? Yeah. How would your family feel? I had to buy a particular T-shirt one time to know I didn't want to buy another. Once the problems are exposed, speakers will go into the solution to the problem—the product or service being sold—and show how amazing the product or service is. Speakers can then answer the objections the different groups of buyers might have; this is mind-reading the objections and allowing the listeners to self-answer them.

At that point, speakers ask for action and go back to their stories to highlight the need for action. Ending with the story gives presentations heart and doesn't leave them with a simple goodbye. We don't want the clients to feel dirty after they purchase on the webinar.

Here's a summary of the process.

- Attention
- Story—real human
- Content
- Offer—ask for the order

- Story—connect with them and make them like you

Here are things to consider for your webinar.

- Make it between thirty and forty-five minutes.
- Schedule it between Tuesdays and Thursdays.
- Schedule it before noon if possible; 11:00 seems to be the best time.
- Promote it three to four weeks ahead of time.
- Send out reminders and promotion right up till the webinar; 29 percent will not register till the day of the event
- Host a Q&A session at the end of the webinar.
- About 38 percent of the viewers will show up to the live webinar; the rest will watch it recorded.
- Content is the biggest reason people watch webinars, so have good content.

If you had to pick a topic you could do a webinar on for your prospects, what would it be, and what offer could you make on your webinar? What objections might your clients have to buying on the webinar? (Think about what objections your prospects have come up with before.) You want to handle each objection as if they were asking you personally when you do your presentation. So if price is one, you would handle that by saying, "I know a lot of you are saying the price is high, and it is. But when you really look at the value of the solution, it becomes clear that the value is greater than the price especially with the special incentives on this webinar. This is not a deal you can afford to miss out on, is it?"

How to Promote a Webinar

A webinar is a great promotion tool. Millions of webinar junkies attend all relevant webinars just to soak up as much content as they can. Promote your webinar to all your prospects for the year. Many people you'll pitch are on the fence or are very close to closing, and a new angle can often push them over the edge.

Because clients crave nonthreatening ways of learning about new products, webinars are the preferred way of learning. I'm shocked at how many old leads I had given up on come back into the fold to view a webinar and get sold. When I look at who bought on the webinar, I find so many tire kickers, people who asked a million questions. Just by doing the webinar and recording the attendees, you will get a new list of old prospects to target, a huge opportunity for new revenue.

A webinar is also normally the least expensive way of acquiring leads. Clients are very likely to sign up for a webinar when they see it offered in an ad, so you will pay less per lead. Webinar leads are also ten times more likely to close than leads from traditional sources.

Those on my sales team prefer our webinar leads; they consider those who spent an hour being educated as serious potential buyers. The only question left is how to connect the dots and close the sale.

1.13 Video Presentations

FYI: Nearly two-thirds of consumers prefer videos under sixty seconds. Videos around two minutes long are the most engaging.

FYI: 70 percent of users look to YouTube before they make a purchase.

Video presentations rock! A well-done video presentation will deliver your best sales pitch 24/7. How cool would it be to send a link and get a sale? A well-done video can do that for you.

This presentation can also be watched by multiple decision makers on their own time in a nonthreatening environment. Video sales presentations are a way for you to get your message out to prospects, especially the behind-the-scene influencers and decision makers, not just the gopher who called in for some information.

I have found that many clients will not take my phone calls but will watch my video presentations. A well-done video presentation will open doors that were otherwise closed. Many executives actually enjoy viewing other companies' marketing ideas, and a video presentation is a great way to get noticed. I like to make my video presentations not just about the sale but also about delivering some information that business owners will find useful. You could even steal some of this content from your webinar script. Being successful is all about leverage, so let one piece of content spread to social channels, videos, emails, and webinars.

A good video presentation will get prospects excited to talk with sales reps and in many cases actually close the deal.

> Effective marketing makes sales unnecessary.
> —Peter Drucker.

More-conservative, risk-averse prospects want to understand everything about a solution before they purchase it. A video presentation can be a great way to answer some of your conservative prospects' unasked questions and unspoken objections. How many times have you given up on prospects because they asked too many questions? How cool would it be to just email them a video that answered every possible question about your product or service? These video presentations will also save you a ton of time; forward one link and you've just saved up to an hour. I love video presentations and use them to leverage and manufacture time in my day. I want to allow technology to remove me from the minutia and wasted time in sales.

Types of Videos

The Before-the-Sale Video

I like to do a quick, before-the-sale, introduction video that brings up the common problem my solution will solve while also introducing myself. That should be the shortest video, no more than a minute. The prospect at that point will often not know enough about you or your solution to commit a lot of time to watching a video.

I like to end this video with, "I look forward to setting up a meeting. Please click the link below for me to share with you the five must-knows for your industry" or whatever your reason for the prospect to book an appointment is. I use this message in conjunction with appointment-scheduling software to make sure nothing is missed. Having a way for prospects to take action after the video is key.

Use the following outline for your before-the-sale video and be as brief as possible.

1. Get their attention.
2. Introduce yourself.
3. Mention the problem you solve.
4. Give statistics about the problem.
5. Tell them why you love what you do.
6. Offer an example of a success, which can be a testimonial.
7. Give a call to action—setting up a phone appointment.

I use this video in conjunction with other contact methods such as social media, phone calls, and emails. You want to let everything build around you so you are noticed. I may send it one day to LinkedIn, then Twitter, then Facebook, then email, and so on. Don't ever give up after just one attempt. I have even tweaked my video to customize it for a particular prospect I was trying to get on the phone by putting that person's name in it.

The After-the-Presentation No Sale Video

This video should be much longer because it goes to viewers who in most cases will want an entire recap of your presentation. The after-the-presentation video will be viewed by those who did not make the presentation or those who are more conservative and need time to think. You know who I'm talking about … your favorite prospects.

Make this video good enough to sell the service. It could run thirty minutes and might even mimic a webinar you've done—repurpose your content as much as you can. This video will often be the most effective video you'll make. So many sales reps pitch someone one time and attempt to close but then never follow up. The video allows the sales rep to follow up right after the presentation especially with conservative buyers when everything is still at the top of their minds. This video can often push deals over the fence. Buyers in most cases have a twenty-four-hour cooling off period, and getting more touches inside that time frame will add a tremendous amount of success to your closing ratio.

Make the after-the-presentation no-sale video your best. I have created these videos with sales reps and watched their presentations in general improve just from the practice they get by doing this presentation. It is amazing the power of hearing and seeing your presentation. We often have no idea what we look or sound like. Think about actors; do they rehearse? If you want to take your game to the next level, you need to rehearse and hone your craft.

Here are the components of the after-the-presentation no-sale video.

1. First, recap that it's normal to want to see everything again before you make a purchase.
2. The purpose of this video is to ease all your concerns and allow you to see everything we went over a second or third time if you want before you move forward.

3. Go over your story in depth.
   a. why you are doing this
   b. what you love about it
   c. your background
   d. a piece about your past and how you overcame a struggle
4. Talk about the problem in depth
   a. give statistics
   b. make the problem you want to solve seem very large
5. Go over your solution and how it solves the problem
6. Show examples of successful clients
7. Explain how your solution is the only one for them
8. Stress urgency to close
9. Ask them to sign and send back the proposal

After-the-Sale Video

In my selling career, I've noticed that between 5 and 10 percent of all buyers call in at some point and act as if no one had told them anything about what they had purchased. They also might even claim that the product was not as described. This phenomenon has nothing to do with the presentation but with the memory and attention of most consumers. You know the buyers I'm talking about, don't you?

The after-the-sale video is designed to help ease these concerns by allowing you to ask, "Did you watch the after-the-sale video I sent you? It recapped everything I went over. I'll send it to you again. This video is really amazing and will answer all your concerns." It reassures your buyers that they didn't make a mistake. They want to see and take notes on all the after-the-sale steps. They'll blow up your phone constantly if you don't clearly set the expectations for the delivery of your service.

For this video, I like to do a screen-share type presentation so I can show the steps and process as simply as possible. My goal is to make sure that after they watch the video, they'll know their first-year goals with the product, how to get the information we need back in (what they need to do and what they should not do), and quickly show all our additional products and services and exactly what the deliverables are on our end. That helps set the stage for a raving fan client.

By automating this process, you can make sure all clients get the same treatment; that will yield consistent sales results and lower cancel rates. **It's not how well you deliver for clients that makes them satisfied; it's how well you delivered based on their expectations.** Use this video to set time and expectations you can overdeliver on.

After-the-Sale Video Components

1. Their next steps
2. How to use it
3. First-year goals with solution
4. Go over solution they purchased again
5. What we are going to do our deliverables
6. What are the client's required action items

This video should not be too long, maybe ten to fifteen minutes.

Jot down some ideas about the pre-appointment video, the deal that doesn't close video, and the after-the-close video. Go ahead—put down some quick bullet points now while the ideas are fresh in your head.

For the video on the client who doesn't close, what should you include to recap the process and make it so they can visually see the solution working for them? Can you show them a testimonial?

1.14 Cheap and almost Free Ways to Get Leads, Attention, and Notice

Social selling makes a cold call less cold.
—Jelle den Dunnen

Social media offers so many ways to get the quantity and quality of leads you want. It's a proven way people like to interact in our new social world. We no longer go out to meet people; we pull our phones out and check out social media updates and new connections. People log on to social media multiple times per day just to see if anyone has messaged them. This is almost a Vegas like experience with notifications and alerts that go off every time we check our social media accounts. Social media is the twenty-first century Vegas it's that exciting for most people.

Due to this intense love of social media, wise salespeople can align their efforts with their clients' need to get notifications and likes on social media effectively getting testimonials distributed constantly every time a client likes or shares the sales reps' posts.

The reciprocal share phenomenon is the fuel that drives the social world. For example, if you share someone's stuff all the time, that person will likely share your information. If you have 100 connections on LinkedIn and every day you share someone's information, you'll be sharing just that one post with a 1,000 people! When you share, those 1,000 people will be very likely to share your message, and if each one has only 200 connections, that's still 200,000 impressions about your solution. If you get all your connections to share your information two times, you'll be at 400,000 impressions. I know the math is crazy, but in short, you don't need a lot of likes to effectively get your content shared.

If the content is good, those connections will reshare the content and it will spread. If you want to maximize your exposure to connections of connections, make sure your posts are engaging. I strongly suggest using video or very well done infographics. It will actually get better traction if it is not perfect but looks authentic, so a cell phone camera is all you need to get started. I got a ton of attention by doing a video jumping off a platform in Costa Rica. The video got shared to my friends, then their friends, and then friends of their friends. The video cost me two minutes of my time and generated a ton of attention for me with my current client base and potential future clients through shares.

The Viral Content Move

Comment and like content that has already gone viral preferably in your own industry. Spend time to search this content out by searching hashtags in the feed that are relevant to your industry. Once I've identified content I want to collaborate with, I'll comment on it, like it, comment on other people's comments, friend the writer or author, friend everyone who commented on the post, and last, share the post.

Many key influencers will respect that you commented favorably on their article and will likely accept your connection and possibly even comment or even share your posts. The viral content also helps to give value to your followers on social media. If you are always sharing good information, your connections will value your contribution and want to reciprocate and engage with you. When you start to look at the biggest names on social, how many just share cool content? The number is high. I also tend to follow all the cool content sharers so I can reshare their content. Why reinvent the wheel?

I also use this as a tool to get people to connect and follow me on social media due to the fact that I reshare great content. This is normally the quickest way to get connections and attention. It's like getting access to the best content and writers in your space.

This technique will also start to quickly make you an industry expert, which will make your sales presentations much more valuable for your clients while increasing your close ratio. If a prospect thinks you're an industry expert, who would they rather have service their account, you or somebody with no online presence? So many sales reps are losing deals to other reps not because of their lack of sales ability but because of their lack of a personal brand online.

Quality Proprietary Content

This is key. You need something you're known for to build up and maintain a loyal following. Your content is key to your long-term success. I suggest trying to simplify everything you do and create steps or metaphors to showcase the data. Most systems and teachings are way too complicated; no one can understand or remember them. Your goal is to offer something the average person can understand and remember. Your goal is to impress your audience and make sure they remember they learned it from you, teach it to others while giving you the credit, and getting you new followers and potential clients.

I have used this system many times and noticed the best results when I combine this with the following campaign.

System to Get a New Proprietary Model Out

- an infographic
- an article
- a video

Having all three together will make your system much more effective in getting your content remembered. Normally after the third exposure, clients start to understand something. But we want to continually hammer the content; we want to focus on using the rule of eight to promote the first three. The rule of eight is simply something I learned from Martin Luther King JR's I have a dream speech. He repeated "I have a dream" eight times and everyone remembered it for years. I like to try to find at least eight ways to get my message out so my message will have the chance to be as effective as Mr. Kings great speech. I may post an infographic three times on social media, I may post the article on social media and email it to my followers, and I may post the video on social media and put it on my website. The more times I can repost the infographic the better. I may also tie the infographic in all my other articles offering a quick recap of the previous content. Remember the main goal—to permanently sink the content—and repetition is the best way to do that.

I know you're saying this is way too much work just to be a sales rep, and you're right. But would you consider doing this if you knew that by becoming a subject matter expert, you could be earning seven figures? How good would it feel to know you have a following in your community that would be there to support you for years? You're building a base with your social platforms that will stay with you no matter what you sell, where you work, or even whom you work for. Trust me—it's worth it. Social media is your duty as a sales rep today and will provide security for your family.

Go Where No One Else Goes

This technique normally pays the most dividends. If you are on media and venues your competition is not on, you will have all the advantage. If my competitors are not using Twitter because it's not the greatest platform for our industry and I can be the only person on Twitter, I will have a huge advantage in that I'll get all the leads on Twitter and look like the dominant player. Finding areas where you can dominate is the key to marketing. Sometimes it can be as simple as a position—number one burger in Florida or the best-rated pool service on Twitter.

In the current social world, the king gets all the rewards; no one wants to deal with second best. Attacking verticals where your competition is not will yield rewards for that reason alone. This strategy will allow you to cut through the noise and build your brand quickly.

The other essential piece of going into new markets is you give yourself a huge advantage if a shift in the game occurs. When Instagram first started, it was small; five years later, it's huge, bigger than Facebook for many younger users. Leveraging your bets and being everywhere will provide you with an advantage as new social platforms take root and move forward. Facebook will always be a large player, but no one stays on top forever. Consumers need and want variety, so diversify your time across the other platforms.

Collaborate with others. This will boost your effectiveness on the internet significantly. This strategy involves networking with complementary businesses. Ask them to share a post you write on their social pages, newsletters, or mailers. You can trade promotions for instance. When I sold Yellow Pages ads, I would try to team up with reps who were selling websites. I noticed that when someone opened, they normally started a website or needed one. So I would refer my new clients to the web developer and the web developer would refer new clients to me, a win-win. I ended up getting a lot of business with this one strategy alone. I used to even promote websites on my social media and offer a free website review. I would bring in the web developer using a package-sale technique. Many times, prospects were more interested in the web development than my product, so it was a reason for me to get an appointment I might not have otherwise received.

Sharing clients and collaborating with other complementary providers gives your client a lot of value. You clients can effectively transfer the trust you established to the affiliate vendor saving them the time of vetting a new vendor. Make sure you trust the affiliate vendors you choose of course. Let them know your reputation is on the line. They need to overdeliver for your clients to protect your reputation.

One last way to collaborate is to trade old leads that did not close between companies. Sometimes, this method will even have clients open to call again. I can give my affiliate a hundred leads and tell them to say I told the affiliate to call because I thought it would be a good idea. I can call back through my leads and ask what they thought of the person I referred them to. It can be a creative way to reopen the door.

Friend and connect with everyone. I spend time every day adding contacts to my network—those I know and those I don't know. I like to connect with influencers and business owners and go through their connections on LinkedIn and friend all their contacts. If I have a large client I sold who is happy with my service, I will want to friend all his contacts and publish an article in which he gave me a testimonial for example. This will add to my ability to promote and convert his contacts since they will be more open to call. The more connections you have, the more opportunities you have, so ask everyone you pitch to connect to you on LinkedIn and other social websites.

Another reason to connect with everyone is that if some are not buying now, they will very likely buy at some point, and social media allows you to easily keep in touch with them. Remember that average buyers take three to twelve months to purchase after they put in a lead. What's your recontact strategy to keep in front of your old leads?

Always look for a reason to expand your social connections and market to them constantly. Social media allows you to build your brand daily with your followers and be there as soon as they're ready to make a purchase for your service or product.

1.15 CRM and Sales

CRM applications can help increase sales by up to 29 percent, sales productivity by up to 34 percent, and sales forecast accuracy by 42 percent (Salesforce.com). But almost all my sales reps hate the idea of a CRM. It's like an instant buzz kill. CRMs are commonly considered a major time waster, an unnecessary complication of a salesperson's job. Do you feel the same way? I hope not, but whatever the case, let's learn to use CRMs because they're not going away. Fair enough?

When I try to train on salesforce.com, our CRM, the majority of my team insists that they know it all and don't need any help. I wrestled with this lack of interest and even strong hatred of my CRM for years from much of my team. My reps would constantly complain that people were stealing their deals. Other reps would complain that they wasted so much time working a file that didn't have notes only to realize a proposal was put out on the account a few weeks earlier by another sales rep. Our CRM was associated much more with total stress and anxiety than an actual money-making device.

My task was to get sales to realize that the CRM was a piggy bank for them. If they used the CRM properly, every dollar they earned would go into their bank, but if they didn't use the CRM properly, they'd lose money to others who knew how to use it.

Within a month after this meeting, my reps were starting to listen and ask questions about the CRM. The final shift happened when I started to show the data on the reps who had actually been using the CRM, and they were our new reps. I showed their close percentage on different types of leads and which lead types each rep closed best, and then I gave them leads based on that. This showed me that some of my reps had never closed certain types of leads even after working hundreds of them; they were having issues aligning their presentations with the reason the leads requested information. I could teach the reps how to align the leads or just give them the leads I knew they could close. Either way, it added dollars to their pockets and saved them time to boot, a win-win. The intel you can obtain with a CRM is essential to tracking and gaining high performance for yourself. The CRM is the playbook of success for you and your team.

The CRM will also provide your sales reps with a ton of organization and the most profitable way of structuring their day. We set up our CRM to handle the organization and automate many of the emails our sales reps sent out. If you used the CRM correctly, you could actually get an account to send out automated emails every day, and that would increase your close ratio on its own. We need five to eight contacts to get a sale; if we can automate them, that's free money, guys 'n' gals.

The CRM's main functions are to keep track of account information, provide a system that links all departments' activities, and to help your sales team make more money.

Here are the key things you need to use your CRM for.

1. Get contacts for next year—as many influencers and decision makers as possible. Cell phones, emails, and so on. You want to make renewals easier.
2. Put in all hot buttons that closed the sale
   a. Personal info
   b. Why they purchased
   c. Business goals
3. Put reminders in to recall accounts based on—
   a. size of client: if larger, they are likely to refer larger, so call them more
   b. how successful clients have been with program (more if more likely to refer)
   c. how likely they are to buy more (set up contact tiers more for better accounts)
   d. renewal time next year

The sales rep who earns $200k or more per year is likely a master at their CRM and already knows how to set up reports to target leads based on their likelihood of closing. I set up reports for my users based on leads that were marked hot but have not been contacted in thirty days; these reports allow my hard-working sales reps to go in and close the people who have been all but forgotten about. It takes on average five to eight follow-ups to get a deal, and most sales reps struggle to follow up once let along eight times. Using the CRM properly can focus the reps' attention on leads that just need a few more calls to get the deal closed.

I also like to use the CRM to track clients who have not been contacted for upsell after the initial purchase. Often, these can be the best leads. I've learned that most clients will invest more with our firm after the first sale is done and delivered, but many reps never set up calls to mine that gold. A CRM can be set up to log tasks to automatically call new clients the day after the sale and seven days after that, providing two contacts to upsell after each sale.

Mastering a CRM can take very little time, but it will first involve deciding that it's important and necessary. Then you can take the next step and commit to learning the CRM. That might involve taking a step back before you leap forward, but don't worry; it's a lot like cleaning and organizing your garage; that takes effort, but the results are then right there for you to admire.

The first few times you implement full tracking and features of your CRM, you'll have to slow down and get used to checking the boxes and referencing the rules of the organization. But after a few months of that, you'll realize you're no longer spending additional time but saving and maximizing time. You will see the number of your accounts lost to other reps go down or disappear and your new sales improve all from just getting organized and letting the CRM guide you to your most profitable tasks. No longer will you be losing accounts due to confusion. You will be able to find and discover old accounts that were orphaned when the previous rep left. Doors that you never knew existed will open for you as well as promotions and advancements.

Technology is taking over selling, and if you fail to learn it now, you may be obsolete soon. Do your part by mastering the CRM and taking your sales to the next level by clicking a few buttons and learning a couple of key reports.

Another thing great about a CRM is the ability to upload account lists to social sites. Many websites such as LinkedIn allow you to import an Excel file of your client list. Doing so will make short work out of connecting with your current client base. You still want to ask permission and connect when you meet prospects, but this is a way to connect with older clients and new clients you're given when sales reps leave your organization.

My IT department does online training and makes sure our CRM is so simple a caveman could use it. But even the simplest systems need the team to buy in to wanting to learn it. Make sure you know the value so you pay attention at your next CRM training. The only path to $200k incomes in my opinion requires strong knowledge and use of your CRM program.

How can I use my CRM to target my best leads?

How can I use my CRM to automate my job? Set follow-up task for me? Building email templates?

How can I use my CRM to help me renew more business?

1.16 Sales Emails—Time Saving

How to write a good email: 1. Write your email 2. Delete most of it 3. Send

—Dan Munz

FYI: 80 percent of users read the headline and online 20 percent read the content.

Emails should always be template-based for sales. There are many reasons this is necessary, but it's due mainly to the fact that emails never sell anything. They are the lowest conversion item in the world especially if they don't offer screaming deals. When most salespeople use email, they make many mistakes that cost them deals and what's more precious—their time.

Here are the biggest mistakes that are made with email.

1. Not using it to set up a phone call
2. Not giving a discount or showing one
3. Not giving a reason to act today
4. Writing one that is so long it will never be read
5. Wasting time drafting an email that should have been based on a template
6. Not sending the email when the client is still on the phone so you can go over the email.
7. Not having bullet points and white space
8. Not writing the email knowing the client will skim the email in ten seconds or less

FYI: According to a report from Litmus Email Analytics, the average time spent reading an email is now 11.1 seconds.

Emails are set up mostly to be a reason for an uninterested prospect to get a salesperson off the phone. You want to make sure your emails aren't lost in the shuffle by sending them when your clients are still on the phone. Focus on getting to the true objections, the real reasons a sale isn't moving forward before you draft the email.

When you are dealing with a sale that is stuck because a client sent an email about an objection, assume there is no way to solve that objection without getting the client on the phone. When a client emails a sales rep, that's often a cheap way to exit the deal. In most cases, clients will call you when they have real questions or issues they want to clarify. Think about the last time you really wanted something; did you hide behind an email or call the salesperson to get the order done? In our organization, those who really want to buy something will call and even go to another rep before they wait around for the rep to respond to voicemail let alone email. Today, when people want something, they want it now.

Use emails as tools to get a meeting with clients, not to sell them. When they are emailing you objections, they are a long way from being sold. Your goal is not to handle a client's objection via email but to get that client on the phone.

Sometimes, emails are sent to annoy and mess with sales reps. I've had clients send me email just to sass me when they really had zero intention of buying. If you get the reason they asked for an email or their objection, you can often start the sale moving forward. Emails in most cases will never advance a sale; they are purely a stalling technique.

Think about how many times you wanted to buy something and asked the sales rep to send you an email and you would follow it up the next day. Not many, right? The minute we want to buy something, we make the decision. Some times when people ask for an email, they're actually wanting to buy, so the time to close them is when they ask for the email, not two days later after they've forgotten about you and your product. Asking for an email is a conditioned response that allows buyers to not be sold something and stay in control of the sales process. Think about it—who wants emails? They're work and drama. People get mad when they get emails. When clients ask for emails, ask them what they want you to focus the email on—get to the objection and try to advance the sale without sending an email. Remember—no one wants an email!

Email Templates

Email templates are a work in progress and should never be finished or written by someone else. Write all your own email templates if you have the option. Take advantage of modeling existing successful email templates, but be able to modify them.

The perfect email template won't look like a template, and the lack of extreme polish is normally the sign that I actually want to read the email. I like to see emails created by reps with some moderate flaws in them. I don't mean deliberately misspelling something, but if the email is perfectly formatted in html with pictures everywhere, it's easy for it to look like a marketing email, not a hand-sent email meant to respond to one specific prospect.

Clients want to feel that your email actually promotes conversation, something they want to interact with. Conversation is the first goal and step with an effective email. After the conversation starts, you can work on getting a phone call and then a sale.

Your email templates should be formed with multiple items in mind. Some companies have a few set email templates but expect totally hand-written emails to be given for way too many circumstances. My email responses are short on purpose; I still want to make sure they're based on templates.

A template is not an excuse to write a Nobel Prize–winning email. Keep your emails short and sweet, you have eleven seconds to get it read and only a 20 percent chance of even having it opened.

Here are some reasons for utilizing email templates.

1. If something works, use it repeatedly.
2. So I don't waste hours typing something I can paste.
3. Most salespeople type super slow and hate composing emails.

Types of Email Templates to Create

- Opening email answered the phone
- Opening email did not answer the phone
- Opening email from an online lead
- During the pitch email request

- After the pitch email that does not close
- The day after the pitch
- Client sends an objection email
- Client wants to cancel via email
- Client wants to ask a bunch of questions in an email
- Client wants something you can't do via email
- General get-the-client-back-on-the phone email

Remember—the outcome of all emails is interaction that leads to a phone call or in-person visit that leads to a sale.

If you've made a video, attach it to these emails.

Opening Emails

This is the email that you should spend the most time writing since you will use it every day. Make it as short as possible, and set it up to get a response via email first. After the response, focus on getting the client on or back on the phone.

Don't send emails that look like spam and thus get no attention. I want my emails to catch a person's eye and get a response; I don't expect my emails to close a deal because my ability to close someone via email is much less than my ability to do so on the phone.

Sometimes, I'll try to get a prospect to respond to a survey or a quick question before I even bring out my sales ability. Remember that often, the subject is more important than the actual body of an email because it's read much more frequently than the body.

Having subject and email body ready to go is key. Write a bad headline and the content doesn't matter. All the emails below are short but packed with power to get a sale back on track. Remember that with emails, we want the outcome of interaction, not prize-winning communication.

Opening Email—Answered the Phone

I want to get this email out while they're still on the phone and preferably before they ask for an email. I want to use this as a visual for my presentation.

> Subject: Contact information
> Hey Bob,
> Here is my contact information.
> Email signature (should sell your services with a slogan; link a video and a product page in signature)

This signature does not have to be on every email, but I want it on this one. My goal is to get the prospect to walk through the email when we're on the phone and click the link in my email signature and go to the page that has all our products and pricing.

If I have a technology product, I can include a link to a demo video in my email. I will use this little simple email to give the prospect something to watch while we're on the phone or before our next appointment. I normally can sell emails as a great way for the prospect to learn something on the video. I've told prospects that I made a mistake halfway through the video and it's funny—"Let me know what you think." Anything that can pique their interest and get them to watch the video will generate a reason for them to give out their email addresses and open the email.

A prospect is more likely to get sold when a rep is not around, and a low-pressure video is a great tool to do that. Let your email be a way to bring out your video salesmen, who can often sneak into the small hidden crevices to get your deal closed.

Opening Email—Did Not Answer the Phone

> Subject: Did my voicemail come through?
> Hey Bob,
> I just left you a message in regards to your current Yellow Pages ad. I would like to ask you a couple of really quick questions. Is email okay, or would you rather do it over the phone?

I trust my email signature explains enough about my company so he knows I'm in sales. He will respond likely with, "What's this about?" or "Sure, email's fine." When he does, I'll ask him a few pointed questions about his business based on the research I did. The key with this email is to see who is curious and use this as a lead-in to do more research. I will get an 80 to 90 percent response rate on this email alone when I'm prospecting.

Opening Email from a Lead

> Subject: Information request for _____
> Hey Bob,
> I just left you a message on your phone in regards to your request for _____ (recap lead). Would you rather we email or talk on the phone?

I like to give people the option to diffuse any fear they have of talking to a salesperson and let them get comfortable with me on email before we talk on the phone. Many prospects who fill out leads are scared they're going to be assaulted by a high-pressure sales rep right after they do so, so they hide in fear instead of responding. The goal is to converse a little and then move into a nonthreatening phone call, a phone call between friends.

During-the-Pitch Email Request

> Subject: Information you requested
> Hey Bob,
> (This should be your only marketing piece email). I have something that has all your prices on it as well as products.

The key with this email is not what is in the email; it's the fact that you sent it without hesitation when the client was on the phone. Your goal is to get ten seconds to go over the email with the client and try to advance the sale. Normally, clients will have unspoken objections for why they asked for the email. We want to stay in the conversation to get the reason the sale is not moving forward. Sometimes, the email request is just an early brush-off. In that case, you have to use the email to ask some probing questions to generate the interest to allow the sale to advance.

After-the-Pitch Email That Does Not Close

> Subject: Professional network
> Hey Bob,
> I know we were not able to put together a deal today, but I would still like to add you to my professional network. Is that okay?
> Attached is the proposal that we talked about for your reference.

Here, I'm taking myself out of the sales cycle and trying to get back into a conversation with the prospect, key to advancing the sale later. When I get a response from the email about my professional network, I'll ask him why the sale didn't close and for any advice for me on future sales. When I get the advice, I can now try to find a strategy to get back in with the prospect. If I can't work it out, I'll ask for a few referrals who would be better fits for our product.

The Day after the Pitch

> Subject: (name of competitor) Have you heard of this company?
> Hey Bob,
> I came across something I think you will really want to see about a competitor in your industry. Would you rather me do it via email or a quick phone chat?

I use this to give him some simple facts about a competitor, or in my case, I try to find a competitor using our program and use that as leverage to close the deal. The key is to start the conversation. Normally, the simpler the request the better; you want to appear as if you want only to add the prospect to your professional network and nothing more.

Client Sends an Objection Email

> Subject: _____
> Hey Bob,

> I agree with you that this is a serious issue. Do you have five minutes to chat on the phone about it? I came across something else that I think you will want to see.

The key is not the objection; it's the fact that the prospect isn't sold. You need to find a way to get the prospect back on the phone so you can sell the prospect on your service. This happens all the time, so find out what works and use it. Any email that gets you a call is successful. But remember that overcoming objections will not get the sale; it will just overcome the objection.

You want to get clients back on the phone so you can refocus them on what happens if your solution works, not just on answering their latest objections. As long as they're focusing on the worst-case scenario, they won't close. Get them on the phone and show them the heaven if they do and the hell if they don't.

Client Emails to Cancel

> Subject: _____
> Hey Bob,
> I understand your reasons and need for cancel. Would you be so kind as to let me do a quick exit survey to learn from you what happened? I take my career seriously, and this would be a huge help to me. I can also finalize your cancel on this call. Is it okay to call you at 4:00 pm?

I want to show that the cancel is done and open the door for some more questions. The key to saving a cancel is not to solve the issue; it's to build massive value and let the client see the benefit of the solution, not the cost and potential risk. Any time clients want to cancel, it's because they've lost sight of the opportunity. To save the deal, you need to remove their fear and tell them it's canceled and then get them on the phone and show them what they are missing out on by canceling it. It's often more effective to point out what happens if they don't do the deal than what happens if they do it. Humans are much more scared of bad consequences than they are motivated by potential success. A heck a lot of people are terrified of success and failure alike. No wonder so many people have an average life.

Client Wants to Ask a Bunch of Questions in an Email

> Hey Bob,
> Subject: _____
> You have some very good questions. Thanks for sending me these. I like when my clients do their research before they buy. That makes my job so much easier. How about I call you so we can spend five minutes and get you the information you need? Is 4:00 p.m. today okay?

I just want to get Bob on the phone. When clients are asking a bunch of crazy questions, it's because they're no longer looking at the solution; they're trying to find all the potential issues with the solution. Get them back on the phone and get them to see the solution working again.

Client Wants Something You Can't Do

> Hey Bob,
> Subject: _____
> That's a good one. I'm glad you asked that. I need to turn this over to my manager to go over. I need five minutes on the phone first to make sure I understand this request and the reason for it. Is now okay?

I just want to get Bob back on the phone so we can go over the solution again. He's not seeing all the benefits and just needs clarification on what he's getting. I need to refocus him on a fair deal. A close you already learned; it's one of my favorites.

General Get-Them-on-the-Phone Email

> Hey Bob,
> Subject: 3:00–-4:00 p.m. today

I'm going to have some time between 3:00 and 4:00 p.m. today and will call you then. I have something you'll want to hear.

Just a quick get them on the phone, a planned cold call. A lot of people will answer the email just because or tell you they can make it and give you a chance to reschedule.

How much time do you waste writing emails that aren't templates?

What is the most important email you need a template for? Jot down a few bullets that you would include in that email now.

1.17 How to Renew Business

It is the function of art to renew our perception. What we are familiar with we cease to see. The writer shakes up the familiar scene, and, as if by magic, we see a new meaning in it.

—Anaïs Nin

Pretty deep quote, right? The message is simple—your clients take things for granted. It's the law of familiarity. You need to remind your clients about all the benefits of your product again when you do a renewal. Let them remember how things were before they purchased. No one wants to go backward, so make not renewing your product feel like going backward. Make it feel like massive change and renewing will keep them safe.

Renewing

Renewing existing clients is something that many salespeople misunderstand. Most sales reps are horrible at renewals, so don't feel bad. No one taught them what you are about to learn; their bosses just thought the renewal business was easy.

Many sales reps assume that renewing business is like a lottery; they ask for renewals and consider the response up to chance. They fail to understand patterns that when followed will yield a higher percentage of renewals and others that result in the opposite outcome.

Some sales reps believe the best renewal system is to ask for the renewal and then try to save it if it doesn't renew. They basically start defending a cancel if they decide they don't want to keep the business. To me, that sounds like a lot of stressful work. My philosophy is much different, and it has proved to yield much better renewal percentages and is a much more enjoyable process to follow for renewing business. The process I'm going to show you is so simple, but no sales books or training I have read even mentions it.

The key to my renewal strategy is to start a conversation and add value to the business whether they do or don't renew. This seems like an odd equation, but this model is key to getting clients to talk to salespeople and allow the sale to potentially occur. Many clients take things for granted, so your job is to make sure your clients do not take your solution for granted. Remember that just because a client doesn't renew doesn't mean he or she couldn't refer you to his or her replacement.

Today, when almost everything is done online, we must treat renewals the same as we treat new leads. I normally prep before I call a prospect and identify a few key talking points that I can center my value proposition around.

When I was selling Yellow Pages ads, I made a comment or gave a tip about something I noticed on clients' websites or social media to start the call. I wanted to grab their attention and show them some value even if they chose not to do business with me. That allowed me to open the door and get a fair shake at renewal business.

Renewals will asking questions to get the information they want: "Did it go up in price?" "When's the deadline?" "I think I may use your competition this year because you're so much more expensive." Be ready to reply to such questions and statements in a nondefensive manner. Once you are aligned, provide value and give reasons the buyer should close today. I never took any renewal deal for granted and always expected every one to need added value before renewing.

When the renewal prospect is talking with you, ask questions that will re-highlight the problem your product or service was solving. This step is very necessary with a renewal since often, your product has solved the problem and many clients might think they can survive without the product since the pain is no longer top of mind. You want to remind them of the pain they no longer feel so that they don't decide to experiment with going along without your product in year two. Ask questions: "Do you remember how business was a year ago before we started?" "Crazy how much has changed in such a short time since we started working together." "How much would your business change if we went back to how things were last year?" Such questions are ways to bring up a problem that has been forgotten about. The better they associate your product with removing pain, the more likely they are to renew.

I like to get prospects to see how much more value my solution will offer them this year than last year. Many clients get bored with a product they've had for several years. Your goal during this stage is to highlight new features of the product or refocus them on how this year, the product will be used differently and produce much better results for them. So many businesses see little or no value in their current purchased services because so little has changed in them over the years and they have forgotten what your service does for them.

Consider cable services, which have not changed for twenty years. One time, I wanted to lower my cable bill because I saw little value in the services I was receiving. I called in and got it lowered, but after that, I realized how much of a service I had and how much I had lost. Contact your clients often and let them how great your service is as well as all the new features that are available as well as those that are coming up. For example, my TV company could show me on my statement how many hours I watch TV per month, how much I thus pay per hour, and how these costs stack up with other entertainment sources. I would also highlight these costs against cord-cutting alternatives. Your competitors are talking to your renewals; it's still you vs. the competition, so make sure your renewals understand how great your company is currently and how much better it will be.

If you educate your clients before you begin the renewal conversation, you'll have a much better chance of renewing them. Make sure you understand your clients and particularly their usage tendency and perception of your product before you ask them to renew.

You can quickly explain to a client who's not seeing value in your product or service the value it has by asking a few questions. Your clients want to have new features and benefits as often as possible, so if your product doesn't have any at the moment, talk about what's coming even if it's five years out. Every renewal call should paint the picture as clearly as possible that this year, clients will be getting more value than they were last year.

When I was selling training services, I stressed the benefits of seeing the material a second and third time, the only way to mastery. Many clients had never thought that doing a course a second time would be more valuable than it was the first time until I explained Bruce Lee's statement: "Fear not the man who has practiced 10,000 kicks one time but fear the man who has practiced one kick 10,000 times."

How can you open your calls so clients get value even if they don't purchase from you?

How can you get clients to feel the pain they had before they purchased your service?

How can you remind your clients of the value they got from your service last year?

How can you get clients to see they will get more value when they renew?

1.18 How to Maintain Business

I'm high maintenance, but I'm worth it.

—Lara Logan

Keeping your client base can be the hardest but the most profitable thing a salesperson can do. **Losing clients is the biggest problem for sales professionals; it's the main reason they burn out and form negative feelings about work**. Losing clients is hard enough; replacing them is difficult as well. Such churn creates stress as well as doubts about the product or service a sales pro is selling.

In the long term, sales reps' mental performance is more important than their closing ability. Those of you who don't get renewals such as realtors do should think about your clients as potential sources of referrals. Your relationship should be so good with your clients after the sale that they would want to buy what you were selling even if you changed companies.

Sales reps fail to maintain their clients because they choose immediate money over long-term money. If you want a consistent, stress-free, six-figure income, you will have to master working now and in some cases for free and be content with being paid next year. **If you're always looking for a quick check, you'll never make the real money or have real success in sales**. Sales is about building a book of business; sales should get easier every year when more and more of your clients renew.

Rule one—always overcommunicate with clients if anything goes wrong. If you made a mistake and the client is upset, call that client every day for the next week until he or she is super happy again. You want to get all your clients so happy with you that they're pitching your services 24/7 and being your best salesperson. Never forget that referrals have a fifteen times greater closing percentage than new leads do.

Rule two—spend 25 to 75 percent of your day on servicing existing business. That might seem high for some, but when you get established, this number may actually move closer to 100 percent. Servicing your clients will normally produce more revenue per call than new business will, but not every call will be dollar facing—you may work for free in the short term in exchange for a large future payoff. Calling clients and making sure they're using your product helps you maintain the relationship and sets up your renewal for next year.

During such checkup calls, you might learn that certain clients have spoken with your competitors. Many times, I learned that competitors had pitched products to my clients but that my relationship with my clients was so high that they asked me if they should purchase it. I was then able to recommend upgrades to their current solutions if practical and take the sales away from my competition. Your clients will earn you a lot of money over time if you cultivate them.

Rule three—prep your clients for next year by explaining the renewal process in depth and highlighting the reasons they should renew. If you like to renew your business ninety days before your service expires, let your clients know that you'll be calling ninety days out to get their renewal and let them know they won't have to worry about any disruptions in service. This is also the time to offer any additional value you can.

Rule four—think long term with your clients—how to make them so happy that they'd never leave you. Every time you talk with a client, you're building your next year's income. The more love you can show your clients, the more income and job satisfaction you will have next year. Remember that clients do not cancel relationships. The time to build relationships with them is after, not during the sale. Every contact you make that is not dollar facing with your clients builds your relationship with them.

Keep in touch with your clients many times throughout the year and in many ways—calls, emails, social media, holiday cards, personal visits, and gifts. The goal is to make sure your clients know you are there for them and highlight the reasons they should maintain their relationship with you and your firm.

These calls will bear massive amounts of fruit. Take this path for thirty days and see how much more of your revenue comes from your existing clients from upsells and referrals alone. And then note its effect on your renewal rate. The real gold in sales is in your client base, not in cold-calling. The most successful and happy sales reps have huge client bases and don't depend on cold-calling, so they avoid the burnout associated with that.

If you churn your clients, you will lose your purpose and mission and need to look for a new company to work for. You will feel that you can't sell the product anymore since no one renews. Clients renew relationships, not products; clients cancel products, not relationships. Learn to build the relationship after the sale and your income will take care of itself.

> Saying hello doesn't have an ROI. It's about building relationships.
>
> —Gary Vaynerchuk

What are some ways you can provide value after the sale and build your relationships with your clients?

1.19 How to Upsell Your Existing Clients

> I think a relationship is like a shark. It has to constantly move forward or it dies.
>
> —Woody Allen

FYI: The probability of selling to an existing customer is 300 to 1,400 percent higher than selling to a prospective customer (Groove)

FYI: It's 50 percent easier to sell to existing customers than to prospective customers (Clarity)

FYI: Only 10 percent of B2B companies' revenue comes from initial sales; 90 percent of the revenue comes from following sales (Marketo)

Upselling is how salespeople get rich, and upselling might be the only way to keep a customer in the long term. I know your concern; you think that if you call them for more dollars, they might cancel what they've already purchased. Trust me. Read on.

The majority of clients chase the newest shiny penny. If you don't have them chasing your solutions, trust me—they're chasing your competitors' solutions. Think about all the marketing on TV nowadays; are you ever tempted to look at someone else's products? Bringing on a client is the start, not the end, of the relationship. I've never had clients cancel just because I called them for an additional product. Trust me—if they want to cancel, they'll let you know. Often, their reaction to being upsold will be the opposite; they'll fight to justify their previous purchases. Making claims like that is all I really need. Thanks for calling. But on some calls, clients say yes, and those yeses will change your sales career; they will grow your income. I'll show you how to maximize these opportunities so you won't be just hoping but actually dominating.

If you spend all your time hunting for new business and fighting to maintain your current business, you'll likely end up burned out and broke. Learning how to upsell is key to getting an easy six-figure income. I refer to upselling as the diamond mining of sales and the only proven method I know for guaranteed success in selling. So many sales reps forget about clients after they sell them or worse— wait for them to call back and cancel for lack of service or more specifically lack of relationship with the reps. At its core, upselling is about getting rewarded for your excellent support and value you provide the client. Reps who upsell their clients get the maximum harvest while reps who don't spend most of their time searching for new rather than existing trees to harvest and then grabbing only one fruit off those trees before moving on in search for more new trees. Sounds like a simple statement, right? But it's a big problem when you can't see the forest through the trees.

It's foolish to let the fruits on your existing client base fall to the ground and rot due to an ineffective recontact strategy. This common issue with not upselling is sales reps' misunderstanding of how clients buy. Reps think they've gotten every last dollar they could have out of a sale based on the trust that sale established. But how much will that potential spending increase after reps have delivered superb value for five or ten years? How much easier is it for clients to buy from those they have trusted for a long time?

There's so much value in upselling, but how do we achieve it? That question is answered by first overcoming the fear many salespeople have about calling their client base. That can be done by starting the upsell and recontact process right after the initial sale before procrastination and fear set in. Overcommunicating with clients after purchases will let the rep start the harvesting process by making sure clients are using and enjoying the products they purchased and quickly handle any problems. I have never called a client and learned of a problem I couldn't solve during that call, but I have had many clients call me with a problem and not even give me time to provide a solution. I'm sure you know what I'm talking about—the calls where clients are just screaming and unable to hear a word you say. Calling clients will never hurt your relationships; it will only make them better.

The next step is to make sure we're positioning ourselves as resources for our clients so we can add value to the relationship every time we interact with them; that makes it more likely they will listen to our recommendation.

Here are some tips I recommend for creating value.

1. Find articles that help the client.
2. Like and comment on their social media posts.
3. Refer business their way.
4. Show them what other clients of yours did with your solutions.
5. Give them special deals.
6. Offer to train their staff.
7. Give your cell number.
8. Show them new ways to use the product.
9. Update them on legal or government regulations.
10. Talk to them about technology and how your clients are using it to increase profits.

Find ways of promoting your relationship with your clients and use them; that will help maximizing your results.

What are some ways you could provide value to your clients when you call them?

After providing clients with added value, we want to go over all the products and services we offer. The client should be interested in seeing what else we have to offer since ideally, the initial purchase exceeded their expectations. If it hasn't, that's a good time to reset expectations and turn the clients back into raving fans. If expectations were met or exceeded, they're primed for an upsell. This additional value we provide helps our case.

Recommending a second purchase is easier than the first sale, and it often yields much higher dollar-size orders. When we first bring a client on, trust is there but at a low level; once we've proven ourselves and overdelivered on the service, trust is higher and the future sale size will be larger and the sale will be quicker. **In short, sale size potential is equal to established trust.**

Trust also makes deals close easier. I might spend $500 max with a rep who cold-calls me, but after I've come to trust that rep, I might spend $10,000 with that rep because my trust level has gone up; I'd be open to looking for value and return when I shop with that rep and spend a lot more. Are you starting to see how much money could be in an upsell? The first sale barely scratches the surface.

When we present our products and services, we should customize them and present them as unique, and this applies to upsells as well. When I sell, I keep track of all my hot buttons in the CRM so I can say, "Because of ____, I wanted to recommend you buy ____ because it will multiply the return on the previous product you purchased."

You don't want to take an established client through a long sales pitch as they won't need it to buy at that point. You now have trust on your side, so it's just like a recommendation to a friend. They are simply looking for sincere, thoughtful recommendations at that point that will add value to their businesses. They already know they can trust you to make valid recommendations and will expect and accept a much more informal proposal. Giving them a long presentation can actually violate some of the established trust. You want to assume there's enough trust already established that when you tell them something, they'll feel confident they can take it to the bank.

I would upsell my existing Yellow Pages clients by offering discounts on ads in other books to buy additional ads in other books, I would open the call with this: "Since you signed up with three other books, we can offer you a special that you'll want to take advantage of. You qualify for a 90 percent discount off these outlier books that are actually included in your new service area, so you'll effectively get a ten times greater return on your investment since you got such a deep discount for the other books." I'd then recommend a much greater program to maximize the discount and often double or triple the clients' spend by showing them value in buying more. This was all possible because I had already established trust with them. This second presentation would normally be done in under ten minutes signed sealed and delivered versus the sixty-minute or longer initial presentation.

How can you come up with a quick way to upsell your clients after the sale?

What is a good offer you could use to upsell your clients?

If you don't have another product, how could you ask for referrals, which are just like upsells?

The final part of the upsell is the close. Often, there is no urgency with upsells since the first purchase solved the main problem, so frame your upsell with a deadline and special incentives if possible that make the offer so good that they'll want to act now, not miss out on something. When I was selling cars to my friends in high school, I'd also sell them rims, tires, and stereo equipment, and I made much more on the upsells than on the cheap cars I sold them. I'd offer discounts on the equipment and free installation if they acted within a certain deadline. That allowed me to have the client close the deal, not me.

Think about the last time you were upsold. How short was the presentation? Once when I was buying business cards, at checkout, they offered to increase my order and add an entire suite of other promotional products. I had spent a good hour shopping and designing the cards and evaluating all the different prices. How long do you think I spent thinking at the checkout cart? Not long. And my sale was likely not profitable for the company until I got upsold at the end.

Don't lean hard on a client you've just sold for an upsell; let your offer do that. If your clients have received a good value on their first purchases, they'll likely think the upsell will offer equal or better value.

Upsells are much easier and more profitable than initial sales; upsells can easily double the value of each of your clients, and getting referrals from them can triple their individual value. Are you coming up with ways to increase your income with every client?

How much extra income would you make if you upsold 25 percent of your client base?

What are some key value items you could provide your client when you recontact them? For example, a painter might offer his customers a lead test for free if they have children in the house.

1.20 How to Fire a Customer

Firing customers is an art and a necessary skill. In all my years of selling, I have had to fire only a few customers; they were costing me much more than they were making me in terms of dollars, time, and headaches.

When you determine you need to fire a customer, it will be based on how much more time you're spending on them compared to other clients and how comparatively frustrating they are.

When you know you need to get rid of a client, the first firing step is the upsell tactic. When a client is bothering me and not generating value, I want that client to buy a bigger package to justify and offset the headaches. If the upsell tactic doesn't work, I continually ask for referrals to possibly achieve the same result, and that normally works very well. In many cases, constant talkers with a lot of time to bug me are talking to a lot of people as well, why not have them push my service. By redirecting the energy of the annoying client to getting me referrals, I may be able to get enough value to tolerate the client. In many cases, simply asking such clients for something every time they call will by itself stop the annoying calls. This is also good practice for you to work on your upsell and referral pitches.

If the first two firing methods don't work, you have to look at removing the client. The first step is setting ground rules of the contract with the client. I normally send a copy of the contract to the client and detail how I've delivered on it. I explain that the additional work the client is requesting wasn't included in the contract. I tell clients who are talking to me in a bad tone that that's unacceptable. If the client is on an annual service contract, have a refund check ready to send to the client. Your goal here when you fire the client is to make it feel that it's in the client's best interest to move on. I'll say, "Because we haven't lived up to your expectations, I want to honor your wishes and refund the remainder of your contract."

If they made a one-time purchase, I'll say, "Based on your feedback and my inability to live up to your standards, I'm going to fire myself from your account. I want to thank you for giving me the opportunity to work with you."

In both cases, **I want to make it clear that I understand the**

clients aren't happy and remove myself from their accounts in a way that makes it sound that it'll be beneficial to them. I try to imply that they were trying to fire me with all their calls but that because they were such nice people, they were just going to keep giving me more and more chances and that they deserved better.

The final step—and I hope you'll never have to take it—is to demand that the client does not interact with you or your organization anymore. This is a very risky step as it can often lead to complaints being filed online or even physical altercations. I have had to do this several times in my career, but if you follow the above steps, you might get the client to admit his or her mistakes and beg for forgiveness. I still always recommend following through on the firing of the client if it gets this far no matter how nice they seem. If you bring them back, it will most likely be a short-lived experience. I simply look them square in the eye and say, "Please do me a favor and take your business elsewhere. I've enjoyed working with you over the years, but this relationship is no longer beneficial to both of us." If that doesn't work and they still insist on coming back, write them a letter thanking them for their business and wishing them luck with their new providers. Written letters have always worked for me; if they don't for you, please message me on social media because I'd love to hear about your experiences.

Firing a client is at times a necessary and very normal part of sales, so don't feel bad about it. It's much better to fire a client before he or she causes much larger problems for you and your company.

What are the first two steps to firing a client?

1.21 How to Sell Yourself on Your Product

> Your most important sale in life is to sell yourself to yourself.
>
> —Maxwell Maltz

The number one reason salespeople leave their companies is that they're no longer sold on the product. When I interview salespeople, I ask them what's the one thing they want in a new position, and it's almost always a product they can believe in. Ethics and sales have often conflicted as some salespeople will choose money over ethics. All companies will have issues with their processes and products. Good salespeople understand that their main role is to maintain a belief in the product or service they're selling.

Getting sold on your product is not a once-a-year sale; it's a daily sale that needs to be done to make sure you keep firmly believing in the product. If you quit believing in your product, your days will be long and uneventful. You will be in essence taking advantage of clients to make a living. All products have faults, but we don't buy for the negatives; we buy for the positives. What are the positives that make clients buy your solution? Why is your solution better than your competitors'?

You need to resell yourself daily on your product or service because most sales calls will involve prospective buyers who will point out reasons your service isn't good. In a typical day, a well-performing salesperson will talk to more than three times as many prospects who say no than those who say yes. Those who say no are often poking at the product and bringing down the salespersons' belief in it. Prospective clients will frequently point out issues with the product because they feel that's their job. That doesn't mean the salesperson has to have issues with the product.

Issues will often arise with the product or service during renewals, and that can alarm salespeople, especially new ones. Many times, clients will say that the solution didn't work for them and not renew and even in some cases ask for refunds, but that's normal no matter how great a product is; it's the buyers' job to complain, but as my uncle Randy told me, "buyers are liars". It's not their job to sell you on your product.

No matter what you sell, some buyers will have issues with it and complain about it, but they're often simply looking for assurance that what they purchased was the correct solution for them and that they shouldn't jump ship. Have you ever tested a sales rep with a fake objection to see if you could get a better deal or just to see how he would respond to it? We all have; just don't let it affect your image of your solution when that happens to you.

Don't make decisions based on worst-case scenarios; make them based on probabilities. Never forget that all products can fail, but what are the probabilities? What is the most likely outcome when the client takes ownership of your solution? Focusing on that daily will keep your sales on track.

Here are some products and services I love and would always renew that I have also complained about.

1. Tony Robbins seminar. Way too expensive, not enough bathrooms, totally disorganized, all the same information that was in his books ... I still went back and still enjoy the experience.
2. Apple. I will never buy another iPhone. The screen took four days to be repaired when it was their defect. I wasted so much time dealing with it.
3. Google AdWords. This is so overpriced, and I'm going to use newer and lower- priced offerings such as Facebook, which is more targeted. I still spend thousands per day on AdWords.

   I have a bunch more examples of this. What are yours?
   Resell yourself on your product or service.

Ask yourself the below questions daily and every time you're in a slump. The more you do that, the bigger deals you will sell and the better you will feel about your product or service. Your job as a salesperson is to be laser focused on the benefits your solution offers and remember that no company has a perfect solution to any problem because perfection doesn't exist.

Think about how easy it is to sell something you believe in. How often have you suggested to others that they should buy something because you felt they'd miss out if they didn't? Your goal is to be so sold on your solution that you're sure you'd be doing your clients a disservice if they didn't buy it.

Questions to stay sold on your product: Here's how to stay sold on your product.

1. Review every testimonial you and your company has gotten. Write down two of them, and repeat that process with different ones. (I email all our testimonials each week to everyone in my office to make sure they see the value we provide.)
2. Write down five ways your product adds value to clients.
3. Write down three issues you've had with other companies you did business with in the last few weeks (a long line at a store, prices way higher in store vs. online, being on hold with customer service, etc.) Realize that every company has some blemishes.
4. Write down three things that have added value to your clients.
5. Ask other salespeople about the issues they have with their organizations. Only do this one time. All salespeople no matter where they work will have some issues. I just want you to be careful that you don't get those sales reps to jump off a bridge. If we look for what's wrong, we'll always find it.

Here's what you can do every day to stay sold on your product.

1. Stay around others who are positive about your product.
2. Keep track of all your success stories.
3. Guard your mind from negative thoughts about your product.
4. Realize that it's normal for customers to say bad things about your company and that it doesn't mean they are true or that they won't buy.

Pro sales reps understand that getting sold on their products is the key to success. A good example of this is when new employees come on board and experience a surge of sales because they're really pumped on the product or service, and that makes sales easy. But when clients start resisting or bashing the service or product, their confidence falters and their sales drop. You've seen this, right? Do you need training to sell your friends on the newest iPhone? Your enthusiasm is all you need, right? You want your enthusiasm about your product to be that high at all times, even during lulls.

Keeping your morale up is key to success. An untrained employee who believes in a product will always outsell trained employees who are plagued by doubt. No sales process is good enough to get reps to sell a product they don't believe in.

Spend time with employees who are positive and sold on your product and you'll find it much easier to keep your energy and sales up. It is your job to keep yourself enthusiastic about your solution and transfer your enthusiasm to clients. Sales is really that easy.

1.22 How to Manage Your Day

Time is more valuable than money. You can get more
money, but you cannot get more time.

—Jim Rohn

How salespeople manage their days is often something no one thinks about. We assume we're supposed to just show up to work and make as many dials as possible and thus as much money as we can.

Tracking dials in my opinion is simply in the mix to keep managers at bay. Are they really keeping track of meaningful activity? How many reps have called automated phone systems or fax machines just to get dials? Are you just reacting all day and hoping large sales slide out of the funnel, or do you know what activities pay off and which don't?

Managing your time is the single most important skill you should master. If you have a strong grip on your time, you can actually forecast your future accomplishments. You can also hone your time in on the most profitable and valuable tasks while removing the less mission-oriented ones. Having a priority and a system to maximize your time is essential to getting your production to the next tier.

When I work with sales reps to design plans to maximize their days, the first component I look at is what they want to accomplish annually, monthly, weekly, and finally daily. If they want to earn $200k per year, I'll break that down and show them they need to earn about $800 a day and then isolate the controllables they need to hit that number—the number of dials needed per day to get the number of presentations needed to get the number of closes required. I have simplified this from the previous chapter on the sales funnel, but you can complicate it again if you must. My goal is for you to start implementing this technique in your sales process asap. We can always refine it later.

Close ratio calculator				
Dials	75		Dials to appt	15

Earning per day	800		appointment show rate	0.8
Presentations needed	5		Appointment close rate	0.4
			Average sale size	500
Value per dial			10.66666667	

I like to first play with the calculator to find out how much controllable activity is needed to hit our earning target. I also want to use this to lay out a clear path to the daily earnings target. Using this calculator, reps can see how each of the breakdowns in the above will impact their earnings. For example, if reps don't have good opens, it will take them many more calls to get appointments. If many clients aren't showing up for appointments, the reps can push the request for appointment on the initial call or send more reminder emails and make sure the appointments are valid before they're set, meaning the clients want to show up for the appointments. The close rate can then be compared to others in the office to form a baseline. We can then work on the baseline for improvements if needed based on how the office does as a whole.

The average size of sale is also looked at, so this can be another item to compare to the rest of the office. Putting together a plan for the day needs to first have a strong understanding of the overall target as well as what areas the sales reps need to develop. I like to manage my day to sharpen skills that need sharpening on the way to and from work but also first thing before I start selling. For example, we use a daily morning role-play to target these weak points.

So now that you have a plan for the activity, let's look at how to prioritize our day. A rep should split a day into five sectors.

1. Learning
2. New business
3. Upselling
4. Renewals
5. Servicing existing accounts

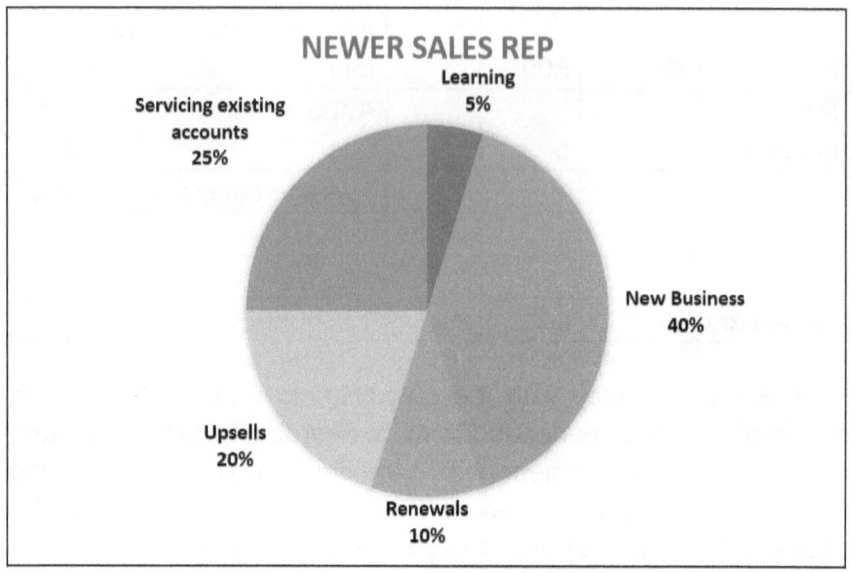

The above chart is set up for a newer sales rep. You can change the model all the time to prioritize how the reps should spend their days as well as where the dials and activity should come from. Having a map like this helps make sure they're focusing on the most profitable and beneficial items. It's like balancing a stock portfolio; if you spend all your time working a large new client but it doesn't happen, you will have no commission and will also lose a ton of your existing clients you should have been contacting and servicing.

This graph should be changed often based on how the output for the rep is and the percentage of existing clients in the rep's book of business as it forms. I've had reps who had worked for me for years who have new business taking less than 5 percent of their day for example. The key is to understand all the sectors; if you're missing a piece, you can expect to run into issues. If you never upsell your clients, other companies will do so and effectively take away your renewals. You have to work each piece of the above to maximize your return.

So we have a pretty clear plan of attack. It's time to execute it. First, we break our day into three sections; I like to do morning, afternoon, and before I leave. We want to assign tasks to each part of the day ideally based on the above sections. Doing the activity every day makes it easier to organize our day and will help sharpen our skills. We walk and talk every day, so no wonder that almost everyone is good at those two activities. Turn good time management into a habit you do daily.

When I come to work, I first role-play or dial, whichever is open to me. I want to get on the phone as quickly as possible and start the day productively—calling my client mix, not just reacting to voicemail and emails.

During the day, you'll run into issues that will throw you off course and out of your most productive mental state, so establish a plan to recover from that. I often save my first break of the day till something frustrates or bothers me and release the tension that way. That lets me set myself back in the state of an unstoppable sales machine. You know the state you need to be in to hit your sales numbers. **If you don't manage your day, others will.** If you simply react all day, your production and success will be threatened and left up to chance. Be proactive every day, and limit or eliminate reacting in the moment. Proactive reps are unstoppable.

How much of your day should be spend on the following?

Table of where to spend time	% spent
Learning	
New business	
Renewal	
Upsell	
Servicing existing clients	

How many dials do you need to get an appointment?

Percentage of your appointments that show up?

Close rate on appointments?

Average commission per client?

Play with the numbers and see how that would change your income per day and per year.

How many dials will you make to new business, renewals, upsells, and win backs? Make sure you break it down based on how you want to generate income from your book of business.

How will you spend time in the morning, afternoon, and before the day ends?

1.23 Call Checklist

Perfection has to do with the end product, but excellence has to do with the process.

—Jerry Moran

Here's a checklist I used at USFCR that you can customize. This one is complex; an ideal one would be much shorter. I choose an example of a large detailed one so you can see the flow and come up with one for your organization. Even if you just have a coffee stand, you still need a checklist. The more turnover you have, the more key a checklist is. Your coffee-stand checklist could simply be something like this.

- Greet clients.
- Ask them for their order.
- Ask them if they want a special promotion.
- Thank them for their business.
- Hand them a customer loyalty card.

Following that process could add thousands of dollars to your business because it provides for forced selling to every client. Success in business is about finding what works and doing it repeatedly. A checklist facilitates that process. Why do you think McDonalds is so successful? Is it the food or the systems? Systems work, and having a sales system and checklist to make sure you follow it is key to consistent paychecks in sales.

Checklist

Beginning—they want information, no salesperson, no wasting time

- Attention/alignment—Make them feel they are in right spot
- Hook—to be continued; what makes them tune in for the entire pitch?
- Permission—to ask questions

- Presentation—is it enjoyable?
- Target—do they know their target? Have they agreed hitting the target is a priority for them?
- Story—joke, client success, prehandle potential major objections, passive pitch all products, metaphors
- Qualifying questions—hot, fire, and closing questions
- Distort Money—trade shows/seminars/vacations/grocery store, 5k, nothing now
- Three pieces of urgency—price going up, paperwork requirements growing, opening/ending year
- Visual piece—email and screen share ideal.
- Next steps—immediate and long term; talk like they've already bought
- Exchange
- Soft close/test close
- Has value been built and tested?
- Hard sell—align and agree, objection—handle, persist
- After sale
- Cell phone—have this for next year and this year
- Competitors—they will get put on the radar, but just ignore them. Ask if they're selling something
- Next day follow-up call—set the appt
- Have you set them up for a larger program later?

If something has to be done right every time, a checklist is almost always used. Airplane pilots use them to make sure nothing is forgotten. Think about the consistency you would have in your presentations and thus in your close rate if you treated your sales presentation like an airplane takeoff checklist. A well-done checklist will actually make your sales process more fun as you'll be more efficient. You'll sell more and have less overall call reluctance, which can occur when you're unsure about what to do on a sales call.

When I ask sales reps what makes work fun, they give me a long list of things. **But in all reality, sales are fun only if you're selling, and a checklist makes sure you sell using the best system on every call.** It takes the peaks and valleys out of your commission checks. Make a checklist for your sales calls and use it on every sale. Your end-of-year numbers will thank you greatly.

1.24 How to Stay Motivated

It does not matter how slowly you go as long as you do not stop.

—Confucius

I never realized I needed to study motivation until I studied and applied it; I then realized that was something I should have done years ago. When I think about motivation, I think about what Zig Ziglar said: "Motivation is like bathing. It needs to be done daily." But I never went any further than that for a long time. I always assumed that because I was an achiever, I didn't need motivation, but boy was I wrong. I didn't realize how wrong I was till I experimented with doing some consistent motivation exercises and started to see the results. I went from never motivating myself to constantly motivating myself, and within a year, I became a new person. I know you are skeptical. I was too.

The main benefits I noticed were a constant sense of flow and a feeling of deep happiness. The motivation increased my output, but much more important, it increased the quality and direction of that output. Motivation is getting going but more specifically getting going with better control and focus. Motivation is the most important skill you'll want to master in sales because motivation will make all your other skills more effective.

I know you're motivated because you're reading this book, but how can you master motivation, maximize your efforts, and achieve amazing results? What is the ritual you need to do? When do you do it? All these questions form the foundation for motivation. Motivation determines how you act in a particular way. The more reasons you have for why you want to do something the better. I've read a lot of books on motivation, but often, such books are way too wordy and confusing. The simplest way to stay motivated is to know the following.

1. Why do you want to do something? The more reasons the better. Do this with everything you do, not just something you need to get moving on.

2. What does the result look like? I mean picture it in your head, what does it look like, and feel like it when accomplished?
3. Who does it benefit other than yourself? Find out the global reason for it.
4. What's the deadline for getting it done?
5. What happens if you don't get it done? (Huge consequences drive action.)
6. What happens if I put this off for a year? What will that cost me?

I ask myself these questions daily, and it takes me only five minutes to do so before I get to work, and I get to work immediately on the most beneficial projects. Answering these six questions daily will turbocharge your results in almost anything in life and keep you motivated to work no matter the obstacles. Answering these questions daily will make you hungry for success and keep you on track. I've done these exercises when working on a large project and realized I was focusing my time on the wrong things. Motivation will get you aligned with your mission by helping you discover what you should be truly focusing your time on.

Motivation Extra Credit

Express your answers to those six questions to five people and watch your output grow. I did this when I wrote my first book, and it got me from an outline to a manuscript in less than two weeks. Expressing your goals and deadlines to others is powerful. Give it a try and use these techniques not just to get motivated but also to double your productivity and direct your focus on what really matters to you.

1.25 How to Tell When You Should Leave a Position

The best way to guarantee a loss is to quit.
—Morgan Freeman

Leaving a position should not ever be taken lightly since it can often take up to nine months to ramp-up in a new sales position.

Whenever I left a sales position, it was due to lack of growth and/or appreciation from upper management. Make a note of those two reasons so you'll remember them when you're managing people. We'll go in depth on how to manage people in part 3 but this will give you a small sample of what is to come in that section.

Even well-compensated employees will leave for the simplest reasons such as lack of appreciation or not being involved in management decisions. You should respect and use your top performers in your organization so they feel involved and growing. Whether or not that growth includes a title, they just need to be in on things.

Leaving a Job Checklist

You must be sold yourself on the product you're selling before you take this leaving a job checklist. Remember that no job is all cake and ice cream; you'll have some issues at any company.

1. Is my income limited?
2. Is the highest earner in my company earning at or near my desired income?
3. Do I have a way to leverage my time? (Getting an assistant or prequalified appointments for instance.)
4. Does management appreciate me? (Ask them.)
5. Do I have upward potential for income?
6. Can I take time off as needed?
7. Am I allowed to work without being micromanaged?
8. Are my sales skills improving?

9. How much could I earn if I stayed here for five years?
10. How much could I earn elsewhere in the next five years?
11. How is the company doing financially?
12. What new products/services does the company have coming out in the next five years?
13. What are the serious threats that could impact my company over the next five years?
14. Do I find what I do rewarding, interesting, exciting?
15. What does my family think?
16. What do my successful friends think about me working here?
17. What do my coworkers think about me working here?
18. What is the best thing that could happen if I moved on?
19. If I stay in this job for the next ten years, will I meet my long-term goals?
20. How long does the average new person stay at the job?
21. How many times have I thought about quitting during the last year?
22. If I got a job that paid the same but required more work, would I take it?
23. What's great about this job?
24. How long could I go without a job?
25. How long could I go with reduced income while I learn a new field?

Your answers to these questions will bring some clarity to your decision to stay or go. If you think about leaving your position more than a few times a year even though you're sold on what you're selling personally, it's probably better to move on. Switching sales jobs is common, but it normally accomplishes very little. Remember that it's your job to sell yourself on your company and solution.

Reps who move on can lose thousands of dollars in lost wages and gain headaches getting back to where they were. At times, they end up in the same trap. It often makes more sense to identify what an ideal working scenario would look like at your current job and try to produce that at your current position. Very rarely does anyone leave to make more money and actually have that happen. So often, people leave jobs because they aren't sold on the product, and when they leave, they run into the same problems with a new company. Have you ever had this happen before?

What should I do before I start to go through should I get a new job checklist?

How long will it take me to replace my earnings when I take a new job?

1.26 How to Tell What Sales Job to Take

This is one of those "it depends" questions. Luckily, since you've read this far, I know you're an achiever, and I think I can make a one-size-fits all recommendation.

You want a sales job that sells something you can wrap your head around and enjoy presenting. That's the first consideration—not money. If you're doing something that doesn't make any sense, no matter how much they're paying you, you won't be happy or likely even productive. The key to any sales job is to be able to understand the product quickly without a ton of research. If you were an engineer, I'd give you the same advice. If you can't catch on quickly or be totally fascinated by it, move on. If you have a weak understanding or interest in the product, you'd likely never be able to sell it long term anyway.

Liking and being passionate about the product is the biggest must when you're looking for a new sales job. Make sure you're juiced about the company and the idea. You will need this passion to flow to your prospects to get sales. You also need to believe in the product and believe it will provide tremendous value to your clients.

Pay and benefits are very important but not how you're likely thinking of. The biggest benefit I want to know about is freedom. Can I control my day and my time off? I also don't want to work for a company that makes me do a lot of paperwork and attend meetings that don't add to my value to the organization.

Now for pay—I want this to ideally be commission only or a very low base and a high commission structure. A top performer always makes more in that situation. A good friend of mine works in pharma and gets a large base of $75k and is lucky if his annual bonus is $10k. The company does everything it can do to make sure this is all he gets. If he blows his quota out of the water one year, they simply raise it. They effectively trapped him with a high base and a BS compensation plan.

Next come benefits. I couldn't care less about benefits if the compensation is right. You can buy a lot of benefits if you're making an extra $100k per year with enough freedom. Everything has a cost—free benefits included. If you're committed to being a top performer, you'll want a variable commission structure that is or very close to commission only. The less guarantee, the more upside and freedom you'll have. A friend of mine for example just cold-called a company to ask to be a distributor of its product. He quickly pitched them on his skills, and they agreed to pay him 50 percent of the revenue on each sale. Do you think he could have gotten that deal being a sales rep for the company? He has no manager, can travel all over the world, and gets to earn more dollars per sale as well than a typical sales rep with a 10 to 33 percent commission. With the skills you're learning in this book, you'll be able to be your own boss and enjoy the rewards that come with that. Keep your mind open and be hungry for more.

Before I take a sales job, I always ask how the top sales reps are doing economically, emotionally, and spiritually. I always ask to speak with their top performers and see what makes them successful and ideally get a day in the life of salespeople there from their vantage point. Talking to a future teammate can shed a lot of light on the position and allow you to quickly know if it's for you. I like to ask the following questions.

1. How long have you been here?
2. What do you like most about the position?
3. What is the hardest part of the job?
4. Would you refer a friend to work here?
5. How long does it take a new person to ramp-up?
6. Why did the last few people leave?
7. How long does it take to close a sale?
8. What do you think makes you successful?

1.27 How to Interview for a Sales Position

- Tell your story.
- Share you beliefs.
- Act like a superstar.
- Don't let them talk you out of the position.
- Stand out.
- Cover them up on social media.
- Follow up—show them you really want the job.
- Be genuine and sincere.

These bullet points will also work to sell by the way.

Questions You Should Ask

An interview is really just a sales presentation where you are the product. When you are picking a career for sales, this is often the biggest sale that you will make in your life. If you can surround yourself with a company full of rock-star earners, you'll have a much better chance of hitting a high six-figure income than if you are working in a phone room with a bunch of drug users and ex-cons. Where you work matters—trust me. If you're working in an investment bank in New York, you'll have a lot more opportunities than if you were working in a small bank in Iowa. Find an organization that pushes you and has the upside to keep you around for the long term.

Take every sales interview seriously, and do your best to get a job offer on every call. Never go on an interview and not try to close the company on hiring you. Under no circumstances do you want to develop any bad habits when you're interviewing.

The key to an excellent career in sales is finding your dream job and doing whatever it takes to get an interview and get hired. To accomplish this, you might have to post your resume to every position available, not just sales. Call in and even show up to the job. The face-to-face close can be very effective. I've hired many people after an in-person resume drop-off. Make sure you tailor your cover letter to show why you drove over specifically for the posted job highlighting the above bullet points.

Many companies are always looking for sales reps even if a job isn't posted. Send in your resume and reach out to the sales manager at any company you really want to work for.

At your interview, first tell your story. This should be rehearsed and demonstrate why you're great at sales and a good fit for the position. Do not just tell a story that makes you seem like a super hero. Your story needs to show that you are a real person and have something driving you. People buy from people they like and trust. When you tell your story, make sure it's the real you. The organization wants to know about where you came from but more important what you're made of.

When I tell my story on my webinars, I talk about how I started selling Yellow Pages ads and working fifty to sixty hours per week being used and unappreciated by the corporate world. I took a chance and started my own company not to make money but to have something I could build up. I wanted my employees to never feel unappreciated as I had.

In my business, our number one rule was to take care of our people. We bought them lunch every day and helped them whenever they needed anything. The company has grown, but we kept this culture. That's why we have had the lowest employee turnover and the highest employee satisfaction in our industry. Every year, our employees continue to refer employees to work for us.

Your storytelling will be the time you connect most with the interviewer, your best chance to make your mark on him or her. Very rarely will you be interrupted while you're telling your story, so use this time to win the interviewer over even before he or she gets to the prepared interview questions. Many interviewers will ask if you have questions before they start. That's when I tell my story to set the tone and then ask my questions. With a good structure, I can handle the interview and allow the interviewer to just sit back and be amazed.

When you're interviewing for a sales position, the interviewer will be looking to see if you can control the call, so be prepared to handle that part; sales is all about taking over the call. Treat interviewers as you would sales prospects. The goal is to get them sold on adding you to their organization's payroll.

Let's talk about your story. A few good statements to make are these.

1. I can sell anyone.
2. I love sales.
3. I'll be your highest producer.
4. I sell the biggest packages.
5. I'm great at prospecting.
6. I'm super positive, lucky, and optimistic.
7. I'm a team player.
8. I go above and beyond.

These are just a few, but remember that your beliefs about yourself will be a key component of the interview, and getting out some beliefs that make you seem unstoppable and super confident are difference makers. You never want to sound reasonable when you're applying for a sales position. The more unreasonable and persistent you look, the better. The interviewer should feel confident that you'll close a ton of business.

Act like a superstar no matter what. Interviewers will always find issues with something—your resume or experience or personality type. Agree with them and say that's why you're perfect for this job. They may say something like, "I don't think you have what it takes. I'm sorry, but we hire only superstars" to push you out the door. Don't take that. Respond aggressively that the interviewer has just found the right person: "I'm glad you hire only superstars. I'd never work for a company that hired low-quality salespeople as that would ruin my ambition and drive. I have to be the best, and if it's too easy to be the best at a company, I'd move on to a bigger company. I wanted to work here because I heard you hired only top salespeople."

When I hire for sales, I always try to talk those I interview out of the job. If I'm able to do that, I don't hire them; if they're that unsure about the position, what are the odds they'd fight to keep the job once they start or more important, convince prospects to close? I want to hire people who see themselves breaking sales quotas before they even start.

No matter what interviewers say, tell them, "Thanks for the observation. I appreciate how thorough you are with the interview process, but I'll be your best hire this decade. Just give me a phone and watch me bring in business. I could close someone right now if you want to see what I can do."

Make sure you stand out. You can do that by having a resume on a funny color paper or wearing a different color suit. You need to be remembered to get hired. When making a hiring decision, interviewers remember the one person who stood out and offered him or her the job. You don't want to get lost in the shuffle of average; think of one thing you could do that would highlight your resume. When you tell your story, this can be a perfect place to put a quirk or something that would be remembered by everyone. An example could be, when I was fifteen, I won the longest pickle contest in my hometown in West Virginia. Think of ways to showcase your experiences that make you stand out.

Always follow up with calls, emails, social media, and in-person visits; be the person they can't get away from. You want your interviewer to think, *I wish our current sales team followed up on clients like this candidate's doing.* You want to show them you're committed to working at their company.

Instead of asking if a job is still open, email the hiring manager a question about the company to show you're still around and very interested in working for the company. Connect with and friend everyone on social media who was involved in the interview process. Read, like, and comment on the company's social media posts. Be passionate about their business and show you're becoming an industry expert; that's whom interviewers want to hire, and make sure the questions you are asking demonstrates that. Try to interact with them every day for the next two weeks. Hires occur in a narrow window for most positions, and you want to be very visible during that time.

Make sure you come across as genuine and sincere; you never want to look fake or phony during the hiring process. You want your interviewer to trust and like you. When you get a job, you're joining a family, and that's often more important than the bottom-line output you'll provide to the organization. Make sure you demonstrate that you care about the people in their organization and would be a great asset.

Once you've won them over with your compassion and sales ability, expect to get a job offer right away. When you believe you'll get the job, you allow the interviewer to be able to reward you with it. Act as if you already have the job when conversing with the company.

Here are questions to ask at a job interview.

1. What makes your top performers so successful?
2. How long does your average sales rep stay?
3. What is the long-term career path for this position?
4. What do you like most about this company?
5. Why do your clients choose you over the competition?
6. How long have you been at this company?

These questions are good ones to ask in addition to some industry-specific questions. Try to extend the interview; the longer you can keep the interviewer engaged, the better chance you have of standing out and winning him or her over and the less time he or she has to interview your competition. Make sure your questions and story hit all the main outcomes of the interviewer to land your dream job. Getting a quality position is the most valuable sale you can ever make.

What's your story?

What are some industry-specific questions you can ask at your dream job interview?

1.28 How to Get a Promotion

You cannot just expect a promotion to come from the sky.

—Jesse White

This is very important information that should be in every book on sales. When I have a management position open, I always get between 20 to 40 percent of my sales staff to apply for it verbally or formally. This is very comical; rarely do employees ever ask me about a management position or how they could become a sales manager.

Lesson one—if you want a management position, ask your HR and manager how you could be considered for one. You need to work toward the opening before the opening comes on the market. Many times, I've given people positions just because they asked for them and were ready for the positions though I hadn't posted or really needed positions filled. Most companies will also be waiting to post positions. Asking can often help get a position posted for you.

Lesson two—try to close the HR team on giving you a promotion on the spot even if a job isn't available. Put together a proposal about your ideas and what you'd do when you got your promotion. Wow them with this detail; you want them to take away just one idea that they would like to implement. This is really not that hard when you think about it. Ideas are everywhere; it's execution that's hard, but they will like the fact that you can implement it if you were the manager. Think of a big problem that plagues your company and come up with solutions for it. You want the HR manager to see more value in promoting you rather than leaving you in your current role.

Lesson three—make sure you follow up on the position at least monthly to see what else you need to do to get the position. You want to get constant feedback on how you're doing on your career path. You also want to put pressure on the HR team to know that you deserve this promotion and might leave if you don't. Never threaten to leave; just let them know you deserve the promotion and want to grow with the organization.

Lesson four—go above and beyond in everything you do. You

want to get attention and provide management value to as many people in the office as possible. You want the HR team to see and experience your leadership value. If you keep this up for a few months, you'll likely get the promotion or at least a timeline when they will award it to you. I have given many promotions out during my tenure as a senior leader. Those I promoted all followed this model.

Let people know you're eager and ready for a promotion even before a position opens up; remember once a position opens up it's often way too late then. Your interview will just be an attempt to talk you out of the position, not a real talk about a promotion. We've all heard the "You don't really want this position" talk.

1.29 How to Negotiate a Deal

> So much of life is a negotiation. So even if you're not in business, you have opportunities to practice all around you.
>
> —Kevin O'Leary

Most salespeople are horrible at getting to the price conversation. Their real error in negotiation is failing to move the client back to the value conversation or the benefits of the solution. Salespeople build and sell value while buyers focus on the what ifs and the price. Never get into a price battle with your buyers; rather, get them to see that the product or service has value far in excess of the price. Never get into a price war with prospects; in most cases, they won't have seen enough value to pull the trigger. Everything will be about getting a deal, and there's no value in a deal. They could even cancel after a close. Make your entire conversation about value, not price.

My experience on over a thousand sales calls has driven home the point to me that the most important thing a buyer wants to see is a confident seller who holds firm and shows value. Most buyers once truly sold on a product would easily spend full price for it. I have experimented as a sales manager and told some reps to keep the price the same, to say that's the best deal they can offer, and told other reps to take the clients' offers. Clients who focus on price aren't focusing on value; even if they got the price they want, they won't be happy and follow through on the deal. Think of it like this—a buyer offers you $15,000 for the car you want $25,000 for and you take it the deal. The buyer's going to think, *Damn. I bet I could have gotten it for even less. Wow. Do I even want this car? I think I want to back out of this one.* Have you ever given clients the price they wanted and they still didn't buy?

After you've tried to keep the deal at the current rate, work on negotiating things the buyer might not be valuing. You'll discover how attached the buyer is to the solution and at the same time build value. That normally wears the buyer down. Go through each feature and benefit with prospects and see if they see value in each one. Through this process, you'll often discover that buyers see value in your product at the current price especially if they do not want to take anything away. I will sometimes even talk them out of removing things by building value as they're trying to take an item away: "If we take away the chrome rims, you'll lose the high-performance tires that would otherwise give you the excellent water traction you wanted. Are you sure you want to take that one away?" This is the ultimate way to build value while aligning yourself with the customers' desire to reduce the price of a product. The "Is this your best price?" question will come up; it's normal, so don't get upset when you're asked that. You can also use this as a way to passively sell the client on the solution again by justifying the value of each part of your solution. If that technique doesn't work, try to negotiate by adding some services to sweeten the deal. I like to call these throw-ins; often, a small additional item can get the deal to close.

The first two pieces of this negotiation are designed to build value and wear the prospect down. Now we can maintain the margin on our product; these could also be payment perks. Once this has been exhausted, we look at moving the client up to a bigger program that costs more but has more value. **When the customer is complaining about price, realize it's never about cost but about value they perceive of your solution.** The largest packages normally have the most value, so never be scared to move them up or talk about how another package has more value. It will also make the last product look more attractive and may close the deal in itself. I have had clients even justify their original selection when I try to move them up; they'll say that the other one is really all they need, so let's move forward with it.

No one has cash today; everything's on credit. If your buyers really want something, they'll be turned down by the finance company if they can't afford it. When buyers say they want it cheaper, that just means they don't see enough value, and there's always more value to show them.

The next one I use is the referral bonus. I ask, "Whom do you know who could use our solution? If you give me five people I close, I'll give you $1,000 credit off your bill. This helps you and me at the same time." I normally get a chuckle and can go back in for the close. The buyer is now ready to sign and should sign.

If you're still having issues at that point, you can ask, "Isn't the value of this greater than its price? Let's move forward—fair enough?" The lesson is to not drop price; that will kill your sales and your margin and lower client satisfaction. If you are in a very competitive business and have to compete solely on price, consider getting a job somewhere else or going in with a fair price from the start. Low-margin businesses do not typically provide abundant sales incomes and job stability. If your company has a low margin, expect it to not be around after the next recession. Start hunting for your dream job now.

PART 2

Marketing Yourself as a Sales Professional

I can already hear it: "I'm not a marketer. I'm a closer! Marketing is a waste of time. I know things are changing, but we have a marketing department for that." You're right—things are changing, but your marketing department should be you.

Let us talk about the best ways to let social media make it easier for you to close prospects. **Social media is now used as a reference check on anyone you want to do business with.** Whether I'm looking to date someone, hire someone, or buy something from someone, I look them up online and search for a lot more than a picture. Having your online presence strong enough can make the difference not just in your next sale but in your future life partner. Starting to see how this is important?

We'll cover some topics in this section that you might think don't apply to you, but life changes, and this book might be a few years or months ahead of its time depending on when and where you're reading it. These trends I'm talking about are growing and will totally change selling. I wrote this book to prepare you for this shift. Sales question for permission: Can I have your permission to step out of the box a little and read this section with an open mind?

First, do a quick search online for your name. Pull up your social accounts, your work bio page, and anything else potential buyers might look at when checking you out online. What comes up? Are you happy with what you see? If your potential buyers did the same search on a competitor's sales reps, what would they find? Could that prompt buyers to buy from another rep?

Things change, and those who accept change move forward. Sales as we know it is changing. Ten years ago, how many people would buy a TV without seeing the picture quality in person? Now, how many people buy TVs by clicking a button based on a friend's recommendation? How many buy a particular TV because it had more positive reviews? How many buy the TV that comes up first in search results? Buyers are changing, so sales are changing. This section will prepare you for that change.

2.1 Social Media—Promoting Yourself

> Don't think of your website as a self-promotion
> machine, think of it as a self-invention machine.
> —Austin Kleon

Why is one sales rep able to close a deal on the first call and another not? Why do clients ask to speak with certain sales reps by name? On social media, you can sell and promote yourself; both are valuable in building your brand. Promoting yourself on social media gives you a high return on your investment; you can create a buzz and build your brand that will yield higher sales. Sales today is highly involved with the internet, so having a well-developed online presence helps close deals. The tactics I'll cover in this brief section will produce a magnified return on all your other sales efforts. Pay attention to this section, and make sure you apply these concepts.

First, consider how your online social profiles look. Some of you might not have any profiles, and I hope that's why you're reading this book. Others will have profiles that look unprofessional, and that will not help them get business either. An unprofessional profile in many cases will actually cost you future business.

A profile should tie in the characteristics potential buyers are looking for with those they want to do business with. So much of sales today is based on knowledge and consulting. If your online profiles portray you as an industry expert and an honest, sincere human, that combination can significantly improve your close ratios. I improve my clients' social media profiles by putting them in the client's frame of mind. What could they show potential clients in their social media profiles that would make them want to buy a large program from them quickly? Once we answer that question, the next is how to drive them to that profile. Sixty-eight percent of prospects go to Facebook before they buy to get more information or ask for opinions. You starting to see why media profile is important?

I recommend having a personal but then a separate professional Facebook page; it can also include pictures of your family and a mention of your interests, but it can be more polished than your personal profile. I often hire graphic designers on Upwork to put together a quick banner ad that showcases a client as an industry expert on LinkedIn. This can be uploaded behind their names and will add a ton of credibility. I try to use LinkedIn for the majority of my social media marketing when I'm selling B2B. If you're selling B2C, you'll likely have to use many other avenues such as Instagram, Twitter, and Snapchat. I then customize my page to reflect what my clients would want to see to buy a bigger program quickly. Clients often want to see a page that shows you as an industry expert who is trustworthy and authentic; you can do that simply by taking a picture at a trade show conference and building a background with an Upwork designer to fit in the upload box for LinkedIn or any other social website. If you have written a book or an article or have received some awards, mention those. The key is to make your profile look professional but not fake.

Getting your brand out in the social world can be a lot easier than you think. Often, just commenting on key articles online will get you a lot of attention. You can find excellent articles to comment on by following industry-relevant hashtags for example. Once you comment on posts, you'll find others you can message directly about their comments and start conversations outside the comments. Once you get conversations going, you can move into talking either on the phone or in a webinar to discuss your opportunity. I have run into many clients we would do a mutual pitch to and end up buying both products. This strategy can work great for B2B sales, while with B2C sales, the interaction is more focused on just getting the relationship.

When promoting yourself on social media, think about how the effort you put into making your profile professional will exponentially help with all your promotion efforts. Posting testimonials from key clients will go a long way to getting conversions. Adding a simple video will further help increase conversions significantly. Social media is growing and is forecast to erase websites in the next five years. It's very likely that in the next few years, sales will be done entirely on social media. It's time to set aside a portion of every day to learn and use this new method of obtaining business. I meet with my salespeople every day by having them read my social posts and learn from me on LinkedIn. Never neglect the future, and understand that social media is here to stay and will continue to expand.

2.2 Video Presentation

- 58 percent of consumers consider companies that produce video content to be more trustworthy.
- 71 percent of consumers say that videos lead to positive impressions of a company.
- 77 percent of consumers consider companies that create online video as more engaged with customers.

I do not know of a better investment of your time than recording a full video presentation of your product or service. I have invested so much time in my video presentation that I often will meet with a client and play my video presentation before I actually go into my main presentation. I've also recorded a three-minute introduction that quickly explains what my company does and how the solutions we provide in depth can solve clients' problems. Having this video presentation has allowed me to open doors that were otherwise not open.

My videos allow me to leverage my time by letting me work 24/7; I automate delivery of this sales video by featuring it on the home page of my website. A video presentation is the ace in the hole for your sales career; it's the only way I know to create time. No matter what you sell, you'll want to make one of these as soon as possible.

When's the last time you viewed another company's sales video? Did it affect your interaction with that company? I often want to watch a few videos before I talk with a salesperson. I want to be educated before I start negotiations on a solution.

I'll show you how to make an effective video sales presentation quickly. When I record video presentations, I like to use video and audio. Most clients believe none of what they hear but most of what they see. These marketing pieces will work as a formal or informal presentation. I use index cards and maybe even a printed and blown-up visual slide to make the video. I record the presentation on my cell phone. I have found that a simple and authentic presentation will actually get more views and traction than a really well-done polished video. Authenticity sells; ask the Kardashians if you don't believe me.

I started with a very cheap and unedited sales video but have moved to semi-edited and more-complete versions. Even with a full production studio, I'll make videos on my cell phone using visual props as I'm going to show you today. I've found that the less production effort, the better the video. Sorry, video production firms. Today, speed of information far outweighs production quality.

Here are the visuals I use in videos.

1. index cards
2. printed screen shots
3. testimonials
4. other clients
5. other people in my organization
6. the product/service
7. quotes
8. other videos
9. statistics

These are some good examples to get you started. I normally just use screen shots that I print and hold up to my cell phone camera next to notes on index cards. On the index cards, I write a combination of statistics, quotes, and steps a client can take to be successful. When I shoot the video, I put the slide in front of the camera or a combo of in front of the camera and sharing the screen with me. Once I get my visuals together, I dry-run the pitch just to see what naturally comes out. It also is good if you can get your voice transcribed on the screen so clients watching without speakers can follow it.

To plan the video, I first address the outcomes it will focus on. I then list the feelings I want my audience to experience. I then write out an outline for how I'm going to handle the filming. I always want to finish the process in one sitting to prevent procrastination. I normally dress in my work attire and just start filming.

Once you get a version done, get feedback on it from a few coworkers. You might then want to tweak it and reshoot it a few times and then pick the best version to roll with. It can take at least five times to film something before it comes off as polished. It's okay to write for the garbage can; just turn the camera on and roll. You'll get better with every video you shoot.

This is an example of a video I did for the three must-dos to make money with Uncle Sam.

Outcomes.

1. Get my name out there
2. Depict myself as an expert on the subject
3. Provide value to my existing clients
4. Open the door to get leads later

Feelings you want watchers to experience.

1. growth
2. excitement
3. curiosity
4. hunger
5. possibility

Outline

1. Introduce myself and title
2. Give three tips (preferred vendor list, forecast list, and carry-on contract)
3. Ask viewers to like, comment, and share
4. Recap content by showing index cards while talking with three knowledge points
5. Explain federal government contracting opportunities

Have fun when you do online videos. The best videos normally have a quirk to them, something that's a little off. Don't worry about perfection; learn what works based on comments, likes, view counts, and placed orders from your actual target market. Your best video will likely the quickest and the cheapest by the way. Being authentic and genuine is what sells most.

Videos are all about getting qualified leads. You could have a video with a million views but none by potential prospects. If that happens to you, you need a new strategy.

2.3 How to Have an Online Presence That Sells For You

To stand out online, you need to look like an expert. The best way to do that is to develop a proprietary process you can promote. In federal contracting, I developed the four paths to success as a federal contractor and the five steps to federal contracting. That allowed me to become a subject matter expert quickly and start attracting leads. First, become clear on what the prospect is currently having issues with and think of some solutions to that problem.

When I was selling Yellow Pages ads, I designed a quick, three-step ad review process that got me a lot of attention on my sales calls. I used top-performing ads in the Yellow Pages as an open to my presentation and said, "I've analyzed every effective ad in the phone book, all the ads that have been unchanged for the last five-plus years. I learned a lot of important things. I'd like to go over my findings with you. I know you'll find this information valuable. Do you have time at ten tomorrow morning?"

I would do that instead of setting up an appointment to talk about renewing ads. My goal was to jump into something of value for the client, not lead in with an expense. Once I delivered value, I could then start advancing the sale. Remember—sales is all about value first.

Look at your most successful clients, take what they're doing, and apply it to others. To develop my four-path model that I used at USFCR, I gained information from my clients to identify the problem. The problem was that two years—the average time it took to get a federal contract—was way to long for them to wait; they needed a quicker way. The four paths was the solution I discovered by studying our most successful clients at USFCR. I used this information to design a process that shortened the time to award a contract. The system worked because it utilized four ways of making money with the federal government. The process also highlighted the need to pursue all four paths at the same time, which was the real trick to shortening the time to award.

This model provided a sales process and customer training that allowed USFCR to be extremely successful. Some clients will even hire outside firms to develop a process and do research to put together an excellent marking and sales piece they then send to potential clients. Getting this done can be extremely worthwhile especially if you use it on every call. Effective marketing pieces will increase your conversations, and a well-done piece could easily double your organization's sales. Marketing is that powerful. As I mentioned, Peter Drucker said that effective marketing makes sales unnecessary.

Here's my three-step formula to creating a proprietary system.

1. Find a problem your clients are having.
2. Create an easy system to solve it by modeling success.
3. Name it (steps or an acronym).

Many of my clients think this sounds so easy that they question if it will have results, but trust me—it's time well spent. Use video and static methods to get your system out to the world. I will even brand some nice flyers with my message and picture on them. Investing money out of pocket as a sales professional is the key to getting a super income. I much rather invest five cents so that when I cold-call a business, I give them a reason to call me back. A lot of companies will leave you on your own for marketing and just forget the value of your time. An in-person sales visit costs between $50 and $275, so why not spend a few extra cents to get a return on your investment of time, gas, and energy? Stand out and increase your close ratio with a proprietary system and a marketing vehicle to reinforce that message.

What can you do to get your prospect to actually want to see you?

What could your proprietary system be?

In summary, don't worry about presenting a polished video; worry about presenting an authentic video that gets your message out in a way clients can understand and makes them want to watch it. Also, do not sell anything in your initial promotion pieces; focus on helping clients solve problems. The main value of these marketing pieces will be when you drive clients to the marketing pieces via sales calls. You can post this system on social media and ask everyone to like it if they approve of your system; that will give you the feedback you want and generate leads.

Networking and exposing your Video

Make sure you network for connections first, not sales. If you friend people on LinkedIn, wait till they first understand you and you understand them before you talk dollars. Networking will often pay off down the road when they actually need your service. I will talk to connections first to understand what they're doing and what they're all about personally before I even mention my solution. After both parties understand each other, I rely on my social posts to attract the bees to the honey as I continue to promote myself and my offerings. Networking works best when it's passive. It should feel as if you're simply out making friends.

A great way to entice your network to make a purchase is by posting client testimonials about how you solved a problem, and they often speak directly to prospects. Many clients have their ears turned off for a salesperson but listen attentively to a client testimonial. If you want to maximize your sales, get every happy client to give you a testimonial and get each one out on social media. Video is the preferred method to capture these testimonials because it displays the most emotion and authenticity. I make it my goal to get each of my sales reps to get and post one client testimonial per month on social media. Testimonials sell products and services, so the more times you can watch and view testimonials the better. Our number one job as sales professionals is to stay sold on our solution.

What will you focus your quick video on?

When will you shoot your video?

2.4 How to Speak Onstage

I could write yet another whole book on this subject, but readers would likely forget all the key pieces and stumble when they actually got on stage. I'll keep it memorable and simple so you won't forget it. The best system for public speaking is the simplest one that you could never forget. Public-speaking skills translate to improved one-on-one situations; if you can hold the attention of an audience of several hundred, how hard could it be to hold the attention of the one or two you give an average sales presentation to?

Speaking onstage comes down to connecting with your audience; if you can do that, you'll become a very effective speaker—more like a professor than an entertainer. Being a great educator and persuader is about simplifying and reinforcing your content in a way that it can be absorbed. You slowly water a garden so the water just doesn't run off into the street but soaks down to the roots. It's the same concept when you're on stage; the slower you present and repeat the content, the more your audience will absorb it.

When I design a presentation, I like to ask myself what I want the client to remember of it five years from now. What is really important? What can I eliminate? How better can I explain this? Can I use a story? A question? A metaphor? A five-step formula? How can I engage the audience? That strengthens my presentation.

However, the greatest presentation in the world is useless if you can't get anyone to watch it or pay attention to it if they do. Many speakers have the best content and are experts in their fields, but their audiences fall asleep or walk out before the presentation ends due to lack of engagement.

Before you get into your content, make sure you've connected with your audience. Your story should portray you as a real human, and it should offer some audience interaction. I like to ask the audience questions and get answers verbally—true or false, yes or no, or with just raising hands. The more interaction you have with your audience, the better you will be viewed as a speaker. If they don't buy in and like you, no matter how great your content is, you'll have trouble maintaining the audience. The audience has to trust and like you just as in a sales presentation.

After you have engaged the audience, you have to maintain that engagement. This is the easiest piece but not always properly executed due mainly to poor planning. When you think about an audience's attention span, think three to seven minutes. Watch your audience, and have tricks up your sleeve every three to seven minutes to retain engagement. Many speakers move around forcing the audience to follow them with their eyes. This visual reference allows speaker to know if the audience is listening actively. Telling jokes will also keep the engagement, so will asking questions and talking about what's coming next.

Content is the least important piece of a presentation but is often the main focus of the planning in a presentation. If you put your audience to bed, the content doesn't matter. The quantity of content is not a problem; the audience's retention of the content is the problem. You want to simplify and reinforce the content embedding it deep in the listeners' minds. In speaking, less is truly more. Less content, more interaction, and being entertaining are the principles of success in speaking.

Put a strong plan together to engage your crowd. Do not rely on your content to be the caffeine of your presentation. Questions are the easiest way to keep an audience listening. Questions hook the mind, and most can be answered internally. If you get your clients or audiences thinking, they'll be alert. Activities and group breakouts can also be a good way to put some of the burden of your presentation on the audience while increasing interaction.

In speaking, reinforcing the content makes the difference in sales and productivity. I like to use the rule of eight when it comes to reinforcing content. Lots of speakers use three, but I learned from Martin Luther King Jr., who let freedom ring eight times. His speech was heard for over fifty years, and it gets louder each year due in part to his use of repetition—the rule of eight.

I reinforce content by framing it on slides and visuals. I use quotes, stories, and examples to further reinforce and content. An activity or exercise with the audience will make the biggest distinction and force the longest term memory from the crowd. Tony Robbins does a fire walk at his seminars, and that stays with his audience for years. Audiences in many cases associate speakers with breakthrough moments, times when they broke through their fear of the fire or specifically the limits that were formally holding them back in life.

Having the audience share their experiences with each other is key after any exercise. Often, the sharing of content or more important the interaction that occurs when participants share with each other is the key difference maker in evaluating how well the speaker performed. Have you ever been in a classroom and had the time just fly by? What were you doing? I bet it wasn't a one-hour lecture; it was likely some kind of group project or breakout session. Don't be scared to incorporate this or even some kind of game into your presentation.

Start adding seminars and speaking to your sales arsenal; you'll quickly realize that these tools are the most effective ways to leverage your sales ability and create lifelong clients. Public speaking is the most rewarding financial experience in my sales career. I have made numerous contacts and generated by far my largest sales and relationships through seminars. I highly suggest you start speaking at your own seminars or working your way on stage at others seminars. When you can persuade an audience in the hundreds, you will consider a presentation to ten or fifteen as trivial. So many great salespeople turn the corner to superstar status after their first onstage experience.

What is your story about? Why you are selling your current product?

How can you keep the audience entertained during your presentation?

How can you reinforce your content so that clients will remember it five years from now?

How can you keep the audience awake?

What questions could you ask the audience to keep them engaged?

What could you do during a breakout session? Could you give the audience a problem to solve?

2.5 How to Do Personal Marketing

Personal marketing is the key to getting the life you want. If you can't sell yourself, how can you sell anything else? How you look online is often more important than your sales presentation in today's world. Having complaints and bad reviews online will seriously affect your close ratio and ability to get sales appointments. So much perception is based on your online presence and especially its relationship to others in your field.

If your competitors have well-maintained online presences, you'll need one as well to maintain your sales. If you don't have one, what risk does that put you at? I strongly suggest that you work to get reviews and maintain a garden of excellence for your personal brand.

I try to leverage my current marketing when I make a sales call; I'll send a request to friend the person on LinkedIn to allow me to showcase the online reputation I have built on LinkedIn. I ask happy clients to post good things on LinkedIn about me and my work. Each sales call I make gets the leverage of the previous work and builds on it. Stacking success on success is the only way I know to reach the top of success mountain.

When you are thinking about marketing yourself, think about watering the grass, not building a house. You need to constantly gather new items to add to your online brand. Your brand is never finished; it can always be improved and cultivated. If you constantly search for things to add to your brand, one negative review will not have a serious impact on your career. At USFCR, we have over a thousand BBB positive reviews, so even if we had ten negative reviews come in a month, we would still be a five-star company. Your online brand is so important, so fortify it against attacks or bad reviews. It takes time to build a reputation, but it takes only minutes to ruin it. Get your brand prepared to handle a few negative reviews.

If your company has poor branding, it is more important than ever to make sure your personal branding shows up good. I ask for an email blurb or review from every client I talk with, and more than half of my requests are granted. Think about how much difference five hundred or so positive reviews would make in your online presence; if you get only eight per month, you'll hit the number in as little as five years. You can take your reviews with you as you move from one company to another if you have them listed on a website such as LinkedIn, and the same goes for your connections and contacts. Definitely worth building a good online presence, right?

I often have people google my name and click on the link for me; that helps pull my website up higher in the search results and gets them to the information I want to use to sell them. Having testimonials and videos on that page allows me to quickly build value without having to perform a screen share or full blown presentation. Clients are also much more likely to believe your information if they find it on the internet either by a Google search or social media. If a salesperson says something, it's suspect, but if a client sees it on the internet, it's often true in the prospects mind. Building and incorporating a strong online presence will allow your hard work to help you close and increase your revenue every day.

Why is it important to build your personal brand?

How can you quickly build your personal brand?

How can you include your marketing in every sales call and further build your brand?

2.6 How to Really Get Referrals

- 92 percent of consumers trust referrals from people they know (Nielsen).
- 77 percent of consumers are more likely to buy a new product when learning about it from friends or family (Nielsen).
- 91 percent of customers say they'd give referrals, but only 11 percent of salespeople ask for referrals.

How do you currently get referrals? Why would your clients give you referrals? When do you ask for a referral in your sales presentation; how do you time it? Do you ask every client for a referral?

Referrals are the lifeblood of any organization, and they are the number one driver of a salesperson's morale. When an organization is getting a lot of referrals, it's operating at or near a peak level of performance. Remember, the main reason salespeople leave an organization is due to lack of belief in the product. Referrals are a sign that your clients are happy with your service and that the reps are filling clients' expectations. Think of referrals as oil changes in your sales career. The more often you change the oil, the longer and more profitable your sales career will be.

Referrals close at a rate fifteen times better than cold-call appointments. Many times, a good referral can also yield a much larger order than what you get from a typical client especially when you mine your highest dollar clients for referrals. A high referral percentage also will increase the value of a marketing lead. If one lead generates a referral, each lead is effectively a buy one get one free; think about that.

So referrals have tremendous value, but how can you get them? The first step is to ask but do so at the right time—when clients are happy and excited, and that normally is after you've delivered beyond their expectations and they're ready to sing your praises. That's a very subjective experience for them, however; not all clients express their happiness overtly, so ask them all for referrals. **Have a set point in the interaction process when you ask for referrals; that ensures that every client is asked for referrals**. You can start to form a percentage of clients who refer and eventually drive a dollar value for asking for referrals. You can also form referral targets and goals. What we measure improves, and we want to measure and track referrals.

The best time to ask for referrals from clients is right after they've paid for the service or product and the sale has been reinforced; asking for a referral then helps further seal the deal. If clients tell others about it, they're cementing their desire for the product and associating themselves with it when they refer. They will also possibly have to justify their purchase to a family member further reinforcing their belief in your solution.

Ask your current client base for referrals; you could get a percentage of them to do so simply by asking the question. If you ask every potential client you talk to for referrals, you may never need to cold call again.

I have found the most success in getting referrals from nonclients who really want what I'm selling but don't have the means to buy it at the present. Think about it—if they want it, they're technically sold; it's just a matter of waiting for them to get the money together. This also gets them off the phone with me until they get the money together. They're likely saying to others, "This is amazing. As soon as I get my bonus, I'm buying the red one. You should get one before they sell out."

Review websites are the real way to get referrals; Amazon does a trillion dollars' worth of business based on reviews. If you took away the reviews on Amazon, sales would plummet. Think about the last item you purchased; did you do research or just trust the reviews? Reviews speed up the purchase cycle and eliminate the long research process: "If everyone's buying and happy with this or that, I should get one too." Make sure your clients see your reviews online when they are in the sales cycle. People buy from reviews alone!

If you can get your clients to recommend you on Google, those recommendations will help influence thousands of potential buyers and likely create many passive referrals. Ask clients to post on social media pictures with your logo in return for a prize or discount. Just getting your clients to post pictures using your services on social media can yield far more buzz and business than getting five referrals if your clients have large social networks. It's still important to still ask for old-fashioned referrals, but getting really good at social media sharing and referring is key.

Here are several key terms for social media.

1. likes
2. shares
3. tags
4. comments
5. reviews
6. pictures with brand
7. contests with brand

These are just a few items I use to promote my businesses on social media. Studying top-liked posts and pages will help you develop a strategy that works. Many companies focus on constant variety with social media; that technique will often move away from great strategies looking for a new one. Remember—social media is about results, not creativity. Some systems work and others don't. Know your outcomes and measure the results. The biggest mistake is abandoning systems that work because their results aren't measured.

At USFCR, we found that dressing up like Uncle Sam yielded a lot of activity for us on social media. We would also have our clients reshare certain posts and comment on special posts for a prize. For example, offering a random prize or promotion will get more attention than anything else. The Kardashians for example got 235,000 comments when they gave away a free iPad to the last post on social media. That was a good idea.

2.7 How to Write a Good Article

The average Google first page result contains 1,890 words.

> —Backlinko, 2016 (https://www.hubspot.com/marketing-statistics)

Writing articles is a lost art in this 140-character world. Articles are something we need to bring back. Reading well-written articles is one of the best ways to learn and retain information. Though watching items on YouTube is very popular, it's often a waste of time compared to reading a well-written educational article. The fact that there are fewer articles being posted means that those that are can get more attention.

YouTube videos show up in Google searches, but articles are still the main way to present digestible data. They're a great way to educate your clients quickly at little or no cost. A video on YouTube may take five to ten hours to prepare, shoot, and release versus fifteen to twenty minutes for a well-done article. An article will last for years, and its content can easily be modified or tweaked when new data is released. Many articles can also be written first and used to reinforce other online content such as a YouTube video.

Write a good article by using metaphors, statistics, stories, and questions. Figure out what you want to leave readers with before you start writing it and what you want them to do. You'll have a much higher chance of getting your message across properly.

Think about a metaphor's ability to pair the known with the unknown. Metaphors allow for information to quickly move from person to person. I use metaphors in my articles and presentations. Your article should provide real value to readers and get them to feel confident and excited enough to make a purchase and feel they already own your product or service. Good metaphors paint the exact picture your client needs to see to move forward. When I was selling cars, my dad would tell me, "There's an ass for every seat." That metaphor has stuck with me for over thirty years and has made me never judge products based on whether I liked them; it was up to customers to decide what they wanted. What's a good metaphor you could use in your current sales presentation?

Statistics are the backbone of any good article; they're the bridge to belief in your message. The more statistics you use in your article, the more trustworthy and persuasive the article will be. I find statistics and then think about how they can steer my outcome and message. A well-done article will mainly inform readers about key items they need to know, but it will also establish the writer as an expert on the subject.

Your article should prompt interaction from the reader. I ask readers to email me after they've read my article so we can connect. At the beginning of this book, I asked you to connect with me on LinkedIn; here it is again—https://www.linkedin.com/in/dan-d-driscoll/—if you skipped it. Repetition is necessary to get your point across. Remember I'll provide some value once you connect, a jackpot reward, so connect and see what you get.

Stories are another great way to hook readers into reading your article. People love stories and particularly their endings. Stories create a massive completion effect on readers and prompt them to finish articles even if their excitement level with the content is low. Stories make it easy for writers to get their points across in ways that don't feel like learning; **we learn the most when we don't feel we're learning**. The most important things you have learned were almost never learned in a classroom. Think about the last great lesson you had. Where were you? For most people it was sitting on Grandpas lap.

Questions are the ultimate way to get your article read and to have an emotional effect on readers. Questions are the most powerful method for getting your reader to experience feelings and generate the outcomes that matter most to the writer. If I asked a reader, "What's the greatest thing that has every occurred in your life? Please describe what made it great," he or she would pull up a memory and relive it before telling me what had happened. Getting readers to relive their amazing experience can be the best way to get them to take action. You could ask, "What piece of your business are you most proud of?" That will often put them in a much more energetic and resourceful state.

All your content should have babies—they should be repurposed several times to maximize your output. An article could be the basis for a video script or social post. The better you get at leveraging and cross-promoting a great article, the more effectively you'll leverage your time when marketing yourself. Marketing is simply getting clients' attention and making them want to listen to a sales presentation.

2.8 How to Network

My golden rule of networking is simple: don't keep score.

—Harvey Mackay

So much networking is done online; in-person networking is almost a lost art. Have you ever been to a networking event and noticed how people refuse to actually network? It almost seems that some people hate going to networking events. Networking should be fun first and financially rewarding second. If your goal when you network is to get an immediate return on your time and investment, networking will rarely work. Networking is a way to have fun, meet people, and find out if you can add value to their lives or if they can add value to yours. If the stars align, you can get to work making this a mutually beneficial business relationship. I know that was a lot, but you need to know the steps from networking to getting a sale. It's important that you don't become the salesy networking guy from whom everyone hides.

I have made many business connections at networking events, but mostly, I've made many great friends and acquaintances. When you are talking with other business owners and sales reps, never forget the value of learning what's working for them. It's normally just one idea or concept, but it could change your life. Networking events are opportunities to find out if other industries or products are where you should be spending your time. Is there some new widget you need to know about? Ask and you can learn a lot at these events. Socializing with other business owners and sales reps can change your model of the world.

How much is networking worth to your business? We often spend between $35 and $100 for a lead, and some B2B leads can cost as much as $200 each. Then you have to look at how many leads you need to call to get a conversion. Just to have a conversation with a lead in today's mobile world can be rare. Getting prospects in person to actually listen to your presentation will significantly increase the chances that they will make a purchase. Networking leads are valuable because they start at the conversation phase of the sales process bypassing the contact phase in the process.

Having a captive, in-person audience for an hour or longer yields a much higher conversion rate than a five- to ten-minute phone call does. The value of a lead is also improved if generated face to face at a networking event. If you are higher-dollar-value sales rep, networking will produce an even greater return than sales reps who sell lower-value items get. If a client of mine is doing lower-dollar sales, we will often look to networking events to sell but also to hire, find distributors, find partners, or even just look around for other vendors. Businesses need to buy things, and the more time you spend shopping, the better the chances are that you'll get the best items for your business. I once met a business process consultant at a networking event and ended up hiring him; he proved to be a wise addition to my team.

So how to network at the event? I know you may be thinking, *I'll have a couple of cocktails, loosen up a bit, and let the magic happen.* That often leads to your getting drunk and accomplishing little. If you want to succeed at such an event, have a plan and a rehearsed open and presentation. Many sales reps have great presentations, but are those presentations set up to be delivered informally? Also, can you sign up business at a networking event? Are you selling an in-person demo? A computer demo? A business lunch? What's your focus at the event? What's the outcome you want? Clarity is power, so get clear on what a win at a networking event looks like.

Once you understand what you're trying to do at an event, you can better tailor your pitch. I find using a combo of connecting on social media and setting up phone presentations normally works best. I like to quickly move into the business side of the presentation to make sure we are moving things along especially if I have identified a good prospect. This allows me to perform a quick product pitch using a combo of my phone and verbal communication to get the prospect excited and agreeing to show up to my presentation. Others will be calling after the event fighting for your dollars. Early birds do get the worm in networking. Set up quick appointments and move prospects along in your sales process if they're good fits.

Last, establish a goal for attending the event; that will allow you to measure how you did there—got so many cards, got so many appointments set up, and met some good people to connect with for social aspects. I like to set this up as a game with my team. We will often split up and work the room in a race to see who can meet as many people as possible. We always want to make the game winnable, and networking needs to have targets and outcomes.

Once we know what we're looking to accomplish at a networking event, we can script the open in a way that will get everyone to agree to a conversation. I normally start my open with a simple, "How many networking events have you been to? What got you to come to this event? What do you like most about what you're currently doing? What are some of the issues you're having right now with your business? What would make this event a success for you?" These are just some of the questions I ask to get a conversation going. The key is to not make it awkward and get the other person talking. Your goal is to find a way to mutually help the other person while having a good time networking.

The awkward and hard part of networking is the time it takes to network with the first person. I always make it a goal at a networking event to introduce myself to someone right away. I like to get ready before I walk into the event by putting my body in a friendly state with a big smile plastered on my face. I then go right into it and start networking. If you seem approachable, others will greet you and you'll have to approach fewer people.

Remember that the more you give, the more you get. Giving out networking pointers and learning about other businesses will make others interested in your business and promotion. Never forget that you're a buyer and are interested in every salesperson's presentation. You're a student of sales, and seeing an amazing pitch could make an event well worth your time.

Last, follow up with your networking leads. Friend on social media, send an email to, and call everyone you met at a networking event. I do that to stand out from the crowd. I thank them for the interaction the previous night. I don't spend a lot of time on such calls, but I make them to prioritize the clients I want to set up for ongoing reach-out. Some of the connections you meet will have no business value, but you'll likely see them again at other events, and keeping good contact is essential to making such events more fun.

I call everyone after the event to make sure they know I think they're important. I try to set up a demo conversation with my A-list prospects on this first call. If I can't connect with them, I follow up again in two days to try again for a connection and then every week till I get in front of them.

I ask people I meet at networking events how many events they have attended to determine how I should handle closing them. If they go to a lot of events, I make sure I don't come off as aggressive. I'll know I have more time to close the business. I have worked with many people who make all their income at networking events and enjoy going to them.

In short, networking events are fun and a great way to meet people and generate sales.

2.9 How to Do Your Own Webinar for Sales

Webinars are a great way to get business, but they are also a great way to practice and strengthen your sales presentation. As we talked about earlier, if you can sell to fifty or a hundred people at once on a webinar, how easy would it be to sell to one or two people afterward? Doing webinars is like training to run by pulling a bus behind you; it strengthens you and makes running without the bus feel easy. Webinars are also the most effective ways to reengage old prospects while attracting new prospects into your sales funnel.

Many times, prospects will have an interest in your product or service but it won't be strong enough to convince them to talk with a "scary" salesperson. Webinars are a low-pressure, nonconfrontational way they can learn about your offer. They can keep prospects engaged in your presentations and allow them to answer the internal questions that are preventing them from moving forward.

Webinars are the best way I know to get prospects to sell themselves. Some of you are still not a hundred percent sold on webinars, and I'm with you on that; a hundred percent is a big percent. But how else could you set up your presentation in a nonthreatening way so buyers can learn about what you're selling without the fear of getting sold? Could you maybe email them an informational video? Could you make your presentation less salesy? What could you do to allow the buyer to sell themselves just by watching your presentation?

To create webinars, I go to GoToMeeting, the one we use (there are others of course) and set up a simple account. You then email out the link from the account to set up a webinar meeting date and time. Think of webinars as a way to get the hundreds of people you have pitched who were on the fence back into the sales funnel. The email list of prospects you have previously given up on is perfect for your webinar. You can even call some of your old prospects and ask them to get on the webinar.

The best system with sales webinars is to try to educate prospects on something they would find of value. A good example could be the three deadly mistakes I have seen businesses make over the last fifteen years, the top three ways to have employees excited to come to work, or even the three things you must know before you buy a product like ours. All of these are great ways to get clients back into the funnel. Remember that prospects who didn't buy often needed more information. Can you remember a customer who asked a million questions? This webinar will move the slower buyers to the purchase stage without your having to hold their hands individually.

Once you get them in the webinar funnel, you have to create a good follow-up and lead capture tool to reengage them after the webinar. I normally like to make an offer at that point. If you aren't able to make an offer, you could suggest an in-person demo or a free consultation. Some clients will be interested and may even want to buy during your webinar, so have an order button on the page or some other way for them to do that.

After the meeting, get a list of the attendees, send them thank-you emails, and call them to ask for their feedback. Feedback can be key to opening doors on leads and starting a conversation about where they are at in the purchase cycle of your product. No matter how great a webinar is, the real money is in the interaction after it, and you want to mine for that by following up with everyone who attended.

Keep track of how many emails you send out and how many show up to the webinar. Typically, about 38 percent of webinar viewers that sign up show up. You want to be able to see the hockey stick growth on your presentation. A well-done webinar can be a key way to get the five to eight contacts necessary to close the deal while you maximize your efficiency by speaking to hundreds of clients at once. As a general rule, 8 percent of attendees will take advantage of a good offer if presented on a webinar. What are your numbers? What you measure will improve.

2.10 How to Get Partners, Affiliates, and Referrals

How do you stop cold-calling? How do you get leads who actually want to talk with you? The answer can be found in affiliates and partners. As I mentioned before, my girlfriend, a chiropractor, had a hard time finding leads. Everyone has back pain but almost no one wants to spend money on what they feel is fake medicine. She passed out hundreds of business cards, but that rarely generated patients. She looked at how many of her clients were referrals from her affiliates—massage therapists and medical doctors—and saw that any one doctor who referred patients to her sent over fifty patients per year to her! Of course she started looking for affiliates to add to her network.

What affiliates could you add who would be very likely to refer work to you? Could you get an affiliate to promote you in a newsletter? Are you able to share revenue with affiliates or barter services with them? Affiliates are valuable, but how can we identify them and get them referring to us?

I never found any good information on affiliates, but what I uncovered was the need to combine a traditional sales approach with social media to get access to great affiliates. Most important was to identify the value the affiliate would receive from you and how valuable they could be to you. Do the math with your existing affiliates, and if you don't have any, do some forecasting, use your imagination, and check with some industry numbers. I'm going to show you a quick forecasting model I have used for clients to make dollars off affiliate marketing. The model has three parts.

Part 1—what is your average client worth? The formula for this involves the average order size, the average times a client buys per year, how long clients stay with you, and how many referrals you get from each. You might not have that info readily available, but most other businesses don't have it either. To start this process, they have to make some guesses. As your business grows, you'll want to have these numbers as they will help you yield the true value of a client and what you can really spend to generate a client.

If you're a sales rep, you're a business owner, so you should start thinking like one! What would it be worth to you to get an affiliate who could make it possible for you to stop having to make cold calls? Find out! You can also substitute average order size for average commission generated per order. As a business owner, you could do this with average order profit as well.

Part 2—what is the close ratio of your contacting or reaching out for affiliate marketing with a call? With just an email? With just a social media tag? With an in-person visit? With a lunch? With an office fruit basket? With a handwritten card? With repetition? With a targeted list? I ask these questions so you'll understand the value of your time and how investing a few dollars to get a more complete plan will be necessary to get affiliates.

On average, an affiliate will produce fifty times the value of a standard customer. So should you spend fifty times the effort and resources to attract an affiliate? Networking events can be a good way to get affiliates. I just want you to start to formulate a number for how many attempts it will take you to close an affiliate and the cost to do so. Think about how few of your competitors are doing this. It's a win-win for both parties. When you get your presentations down, you'll likely use it as your main lead capture method. A fifty-to-one return sounds pretty good to me.

Part 3—what should you give potential affiliates as an incentive for becoming affiliates? What would make them want to do business with you? Why would they email your information to their clients? This can be a lot of different things, but the key is to offer something. You could simply offer a kickback of 10 percent of your commission or a flat $50 per sale. The average lead costs between $35 and $100, and the close rate is not 100 percent on them. But if you used this math, you could likely pay $100 per closed deal and still make a lot of money with affiliates.

I consider affiliates to be a form of free advertising and a way to get leads that builds trust between us. When I pitch an affiliate, normally, a reciprocating idea can work well and cost nothing. My girlfriend could keep a massage therapist's business cards by her register and the massage therapist could do the same. That would be an entry-level affiliation; an advanced program could involve a greater integration of businesses. Some businesses that are low profit but have thousands of clients could make more money with affiliate programs than they make in their actual businesses. One restaurant collected business cards and would draw them for a free trip to a time-share resort. The restaurant owner received a 25 percent revenue share of anyone he sent who bought a time share. That process generated more money than the struggling owner was making with the restaurant.

Who could you form affiliate relationships with? When I sold advertising, I wanted to establish relationships with other advertising reps. A friend who worked for a competitor would sell a client and then flip the lead to me. We traded leads back and forth and helped clients get advertising they were going to purchase in the yellowpages we both sold anyway, and both of us got commissions. This trick saved us a lot of cold-calling.

Average Value of Affiliate	Close Ratio on Affiliate	Cost of Offer to Affiliate

What's the quick and easy process to get an affiliate?

1. Come up with a list of the best companies that could refer you work.
2. Set up a strategy using social media, calls, letters, in-person visits, lunches, networking events, gift baskets, and repetition.
3. Plan a good opening; have an irresistible offer in it: "I have a way for you to add $100k per year to your business without risk. Can I have five minutes of your time to go over it? I promise I'm not selling anything. You have to hear this."
4. Track the results of leads, conversations, closes, and value per referral source.
5. Reward your affiliates fairly; once you start working with them, the competition might try to steal your idea.

PART 3

Sales Management— How to Become a Sales Manager and More Important Manage Yourself

What is sales management? What does it mean to be a sales manager? Do I need to learn to be a sales manager even if I'm only going to be a sales rep? I asked these questions when I started selling cars for my father at age fifteen. Finding the answers seemed easy at the time, but it took me many years to really understand the answers and more time to integrate them into my selling career.

The first question, What is sales management? is often addressed from the frame of busting balls. Most sales reps don't love their sales managers, so modeling a bad manager is not a good way to become a great manager. Think of the sales manager you had that made a difference in your life, the one you will never forget. What were the characteristics of that manager? How did that manager lead? How did that manager give orders to the team? What was the one thing he or she did that made you like him or her so much? You're coming up with a picture of a great manager.

Jot down a few things you'd emulate if you were a sales manager.

Write down some key traits of a great sales manger

Now that you captured some key traits of leadership, I want to tell you about my favorite sales manager, Neil. He was an older Kentucky gentleman who was honest, direct, and sincere. He cared deeply about our team and especially helping us advance. He was always patient and understanding; he always did the right thing. He was the glue that held the team together so much that we didn't look for work elsewhere. His team was so strong that every member was willing to lead. Neil didn't have to lead because he built a team of leaders.

When a problem arose that affected the team, Neil made sure we all knew it was normal and felt thankful that this was the only thing coming. He framed setbacks by reminding us of how much worse it could have been and by showing that together, we could get through anything. He did this in a sincere way by talking about some challenges he'd had in his years. He shed positive light on everything that happened in the organization.

Spending fifteen minutes with him would leave me feeling alive and rejuvenated. One talk with Neil would elevate your life, not just your sales. It was easy to see that he cared about us personally, not just our production. He was a numbers guy who understood it was his reps who produced the numbers.

A good sales manager is a lot like Neil. Providing numbers and spreadsheets are necessary in a high-performance culture, but the main job of a sales manager is to hold the team together and get its members to work on their sales goals and realize the amazing qualities of what they were selling and how lucky they were to be working together.

I'll go into some concepts that will make you a good sales manager. I know you're asking, "Should I really read this? I mean, don't sales managers make less money? Doesn't everyone hate sales managers? And I already know how to manage." I feel your concerns, but I promise this section will deliver more value than the other two sections combined. So are you with me?

You need to learn to be a sales manager because that will allow you to perform in your current position at a higher level. Oh, and it'll keep your current sales manager off your back. Becoming a sales manager should be a goal of every sales rep, and it may not necessarily be about becoming one at your current company. That's because many salespeople can transition to business owners easily; if you can sell it, you can always find someone to produce it. And sales reps effectively have their own businesses especially if they can renew their current clients. What I'll explain in this part will allow you to better manage yourself and increase your efficiency. **Remember that if you control how much money you earn, you have your own business. Never forget that, fellow business owner!**

My goal in this part of the book is to make sure you learn to live a life with no limits. You can be the person who turns down a promotion if you choose. To put a management position in perspective, it can take up to five years of demonstrating the skills we'll go over to just be offered a sales manager promotion. If you don't have perfect optics on five years out, read this with an open mind; I promise it'll be worthwhile. Learning the skills to manage yourself is essential in today's world of remote work. Gaining management experience is even becoming a requirement for many competitive sales roles. Current sales managers, take notes—much information in this book isn't available anywhere else, so yes, there is value for you here. Read on!

What were the traits of the good managers you've had?

What made them great?

What did they do to motivate you?

3.1 Why You Need to Be a Leader

What really defines a leader in today's world? Who needs to be a leader in an organization? Is the person with the title really the leader? Who does the team go to for advice and guidance?

The person with the title of manager is often not the leader of the organization. In many organizations, the leader is the one who leads the team to make tough decisions. If a company rolled out something that was going to reduce sales commissions, would you expect your manager to shed light on your decision to stay or leave the organization, or would you go to someone else in the company for advice? In our current culture, leadership does not come only from coworkers; many are led by people on social media or even high-level masterminds. Those people will be more interested in checking with such mentors than with leaders at the office.

If you are a manager, there may be several members on your team who help you lead. You'll lead in certain matters, but in others, you might not be the leader. Leadership involves having multiple key members who will reinforce your message; they'll be like remote speakers that will get your message out to the entire organization.

When a leader is away or not able to lead, who leads? Great managers always build strong leaders under themselves to serve when they are away and in particular to rise to the occasion when chaos strikes. These leaders are ready to step in permanently or temporarily; they're leaders on the bench so to speak. Leaders are those whom the team trusts to represent their interests. Leaders in most cases are those with the most energy, passion, skill, tenure, or any combo of these qualities, but this is not always the case. Ken Blanchard said that a good leader was a servant leader, one who served the needs of the team. How could you better serve the needs of your team both as a manager and not as a manger?

An organization that is growing and setting the standard for its industry will need every player on the team to be a leader, and not just a leader but a growing leader, one who could take an executive position when one became available. Leadership can't be done by one person; it needs to be done by everyone. When a team is operating at its peak, everyone is going above and beyond and keeping the energy, morale, and mission of the team at the forefront of everyone's mind.

When you are acting as a leader, you'll feel better about your work, you'll have more energy, and you'll start making more money. You'll feel more fulfilled, and you will expand and be able to lead whether at your current company, another one, or one you establish. You have a bright future, so take the first step today to get there.

Leadership is a passion of mine. Until I started leading without the title, I never had a desire to be a leader. I had always viewed managers as babysitters who earned less than a great salesperson did. Boy was I wrong. Leaders can be great assets to a team; they can hold it together. Remove a great leader and the team will slowly unravel. Add a great leader and watch the culture and energy of the team rise.

3.2 How to Be a Sales Manager

What really makes a great sales manager? How does one get selected to be a sales manager? What does a sales manager really do? Should I be a sales manager? How did the current managers get promoted?

When I first got into sales, I wanted to find out how and why someone got promoted to the position of sales manager. I had heard they made less money and had to deal with more drama. I asked coworkers and anyone who would listen to me. To my surprise, the answers I received didn't match up. Some managers said they were promoted when the office expanded. Some said they were promoted when someone quit. Some said it was due to someone being fired. Others said it was because they had experience managing.

The answers were cloudy to say the least. I was fortunately able to uncover a few things from fellow sales reps that seemed to align and form a congruent truth. The best reps were not those who became sales managers; those who were promoted were average reps who seemed to get along with everyone—nice people who could appreciate the performance of superstars and be compassionate with underperformers. These managers were much more willing to help out around the office than to hit their sales targets.

When I worked at Verizon for example, none of the sales managers had ever been award winners, but they were nice to the other managers in the office as well as the general manager.

So should you be a sales manager? The answer depends on you as a person and your long-term goals. If you want to lead and develop people, absolutely. If you want to make as much money as possible, becoming a manager might not be for you. On average, sales managers make 30 percent less than their top reps do and have to work more hours.

A good candidate for a sales manager position likes to coach and develop others so much that they might even do so for free. Being a leader is something you should enjoy doing so much that you'll work harder for the position and be willing to make less money and deal with countless reports. The feeling I get when I help someone grow has been worth any sacrifice I've made to do so. Being on a winning team is huge, but the sense of joy you get by assembling that team is priceless. Develop your leadership skills no matter what path you choose to ultimately take, remember you always want to be a leader whether you have or don't have the title.

To be a good sales manager, you need to address my three rules of management: identify the key metrics of your position, measure and communicate them daily and weekly, and develop leaders on your team. When I teach this to new managers, they think, *Duh! This sounds so simple*, and it really is. The simplest things separate those who excel from those who fail. Success is simply doing the right things consistently.

Let's go over the simple things you need to do be a great sales manager. The first is to identify the key metrics or drivers of your position. Key metrics for a sales position will center on how leads come in as well as how your sales process closes. When we look for metrics, we're looking for the progress points of a sale. Typically, a lead is given or dialed. Then that lead will have a conversation and be sold or agree to an appointment. The lead will show or not show for the appointment. Then comes the solution recommendation phase, and then a sale will either occur or not. Then comes the reengagement on the sale. If the sale doesn't close, then there will be follow-up with the prospect to try to reengage the sale. I know—I lost you, but don't worry ... it'll get easier.

Let's take a closer look at each phase and establish a way to record the most important pieces of the sales process. As I walk you through the sales process I used at USFCR, think about your sales process and mirror and adapt it to fit yours. At USFCR, all our leads came from our website or phone calls to our firm. No matter what you sell, you'll notice a process very similar to the one above. I have even used this process for a food truck.

I'm going to address website leads first since that will be most applicable to the majority of companies. Sit up and take a deep breath; this is information that will change your sales career. People would go to the USFCR website and fill out a form to learn more about federal contracting. The forms were assigned to salespeople, who would call and email the potential clients to have conversations and uncover their pain points and reasons to advance the sale. The clients would answer or not answer the phone. If they didn't answer, we'd email them or set an appointment for a recall. Are you starting to see some holes in your lead contact process already? Good sales managers want to measure each spot in the process to find out which team members are strong and which are weak. You can also see how the pieces work together. Let me show you what I uncovered from tracking my sales process.

The first question I asked

What are some reasons that could affect whether a prospect answers the phone? When I asked this question, I noticed some things right away. Some of my reps were far better, like 300 percent better, at getting conversations with leads than were other reps, who were not my high earners. When I observed these high conversation starters, I noticed the first golden nugget—**the reps who called quickly had a higher rate of leads to conversation.** If I got all my reps to follow this same model, that would equate to a potential 300 percent increase in sales without the addition of another lead. Interesting, right?

I also learned that these reps had a way of getting the decision makers on the phone. **They knew how to remind those who filled out the lead form that they really wanted to take this sales call**. They also in most cases sent emails that created a sense of urgency. And they called multiple times with extra focus on calling quickly the first day.

The next costly falloff happened when reps made contact and booked appointments to perform the sales presentation. Missed appointments will waste a ton of sales reps' time, easily an hour for each one. To cut down on missed appointments, my top reps were sending out simple calendar invites and driving home the point with the leads that reminded them they were setting aside time for them. They would ask the leads to let them know ahead of time if something conflicted with the set-aside time asap. That simple step could increase the number of presentations you could deliver in a day by 70 percent. The math doesn't lie. If 70 percent more clients showed up for presentations and you kept your sales close rate, you'd have 233 percent more sales. Ready to learn more?

The numbers told me that a small percentage of reps who didn't have many scheduled appointments still sold a ton. Those reps were pushing through the appointment and asking questions, including, "What would you like me to focus on?" The answer allowed them to clarify the matter and move into a needs analysis. The reps kept asking questions to advance the sale until the prospect was interested enough to reenter the sales process. The reps were not willing to set up an appointment unless they had to. The reps knew that "Call me later" was an automatic response in most cases and not a hard objection. In the needs-analysis phase, the reps were in most cases easily able to continue the call or at least get leads interested in attending the appointments. This is the intel you need to master sales.

Business owners never have time to speak with salespeople and especially those who don't have something really good to tell them. Getting clarification on what the prospect wants the sales rep to go over in the meeting is essential to getting the prospect to show up to that meeting. This preappointment conversation allows reps to learn and deliver what the prospects want to hear in the sales presentation. In many cases, this will allow sales reps to earn the right for more time on the sales call and in many cases advance the call without waiting for appointments. Using this technique can increase your reps' close ratio up to 50 percent and decrease your sales process by several days. I have had reps who have had over 70 percent no-show rates on appointments. How do you think this data would help them?

The next big falloff point is the presentation. Think about all the steps we have gone through before we even get to the main sales presentation. When you're a sales manager, you'll start to uncover ways to coach your top performers and remove inefficiencies in their sales process. To really move them to the next level of performance, managers will have to make small tweaks, but they first have to know where the falloff points are.

Before we can coach reps, we have to see something that needs improving. They will be blown away in many cases when they see a metric that shows they're not number one. Showing this metric stacking the performance of each of your reps against a top performer will get their attention. Once you have their attention, they'll likely be more open to coaching and want to improve. Can you see how that would help you in your sales career?

Let's recap while your brain is ready to learn.

- Measure each level of your performance
  - Leads
  - Dials
  - Conversations
  - Appointments
  - Presentations
  - Proposals
    - Plus average size of proposal
  - Closes
  - Reengagement
- Rank your team against each other
  - Find out the leaders in each segment and model them.
  - Make it competitive between each person.
  - Reward and recognize the winners.
- Coach your team where they need it.
  - Let your team members coach each other.

The conversation is the longest part of the sales process and has the most steps. When you're training new reps, getting the sales process down is important, but without the conversation, you have nothing; it's the essential piece in the sales process. We aren't going to dive into the sales process again since we covered that in the first part, but know that this is the only place most sales managers coach. Coaching only on the conversation or presentation is like working your body out by doing only curls. You'll end up looking very out of proportion and will not likely win many body-building competitions.

The biggest issue I noticed in the conversation phase was not asking the proper questions. You get prospects to listen to the entire sales presentation and keep them from checking out by asking engaging questions. Think about what questions your reps should ask during every presentation, and make sure they know them and ask them on every call.

In our business, the separator between reps who go out on a

lot of proposals was simply whether they used screen share. In our business, in which we sold over the phone, keeping potential clients' attention was hard, but by using screen share, we were able to keep them engaged and participating in the sales presentation all the way to the proposal phase. After you get a proposal the next step is? Yep, a conversion or a signed contract.

Who's your best closer? Being a closer is great. But if you fail at any of the first steps—from getting prospects on the phone and having conversations with them to making a presentation, you won't get a signed deal. However, and very important, the signed deal is *not* the next step. The next step is average size of proposal out. If you have a sales rep who pitches only $400 deals and all your other reps propose $1,000 deals, what could that tell you? How would that affect the sales for that rep? Is that rep selling out of his pocket? Does he have a fear of asking for large orders? So the next number to track is average proposal size. How much money will reps leave on the table if they fail to ask for what the client really needs?

A lot of sales reps are scared or have limiting beliefs about asking for orders over a certain size. Maybe the rep worked at a company for ten years where the biggest sale ever was $400 and he thinks he can't sell any more than that. This is a very common issue in sales; the only cure is to train how to tell what the client needs and to recommend around client needs, not the rep's feelings. In our industry, we ask questions to base proposal size on what the client qualifies for, and we pitch all clients on that. If a client has issues with the price, we can always adjust it later if needed, but we want clients to tell us what they can or can't afford, not the sales rep. This is a huge problem in sales. This one simple limiting belief can cost reps hundreds of thousands of dollars over their sales careers.

Sales leaders want to make sure their reps have systems to tell them what to recommend to each client. **I always want to reinforce to my reps that the larger the programs clients buy are, the more likely they are to use them, get value from them, and thus be happy with them.** I have always noticed the lowest satisfaction ratings with the cheapest programs. It's like buying the base Corolla with hand-crank windows and no air conditioning when you live in Florida. Lower end products have a limit to how much satisfaction clients can get from them. The best products remove the limits and let clients have the true full experience. Clients will often forget about the price but not the lack of features and the poor ownership experience.

If you're selling cars, for instance, you could ask customers a set list of questions about all the features of the car and based on their responses recommend the premium options. "Do you plan to drive this car a lot in the winter?" If the client says yes, you recommend the winter package. A rep for a lawn spray company could ask, "How long do you plan on keeping your home?" If the client says five years, the rep could pitch a five-year program at a locked-in rate. What questions could you put together to give clarity to your sales reps on what to recommend to clients? If you don't give instructions to your sales team, your numbers will be all over the place and you'll be dropping the ball.

The consistency of the numbers a sales team produces is the main gauge of the manager's effectiveness. Don't leave your team's proposal size numbers up to chance. Take the risk out and have a system that determines how much each sales rep asks clients for. Starting to see how you could make your team more consistent?

The last item that we will view will be conversions—proposals to closed deals. Conversions are simply not that important in my opinion. It's much more important to do the first parts of this process correctly than to neglect them in exchange for a better close rate. If I close one out of three and get a hundred closing opportunities per week, I'll close thirty-three. Another rep might close two out of three, but if he gets only thirty closing opportunities a week, he'll close just twenty. Many times when I have viewed top closers, I found out that they spent so much time on the phone that they claimed that was why they had little activity. The time on the phone in all my experience is not the issue; it's that they feel they can't make the extra dials. They feel that closers shouldn't have to dial, and they pride themselves on having a high close ratio. Some sales reps I've worked with don't even want to take a lot of leads because they want to keep their close percentage up. That's a limiting belief that needs to be removed. What other limiting beliefs may be holding back your team?

What did I notice that allowed one rep in our firm to close twice as much as another rep? Very simple—he stayed cool when a client objected. The top closer actually liked the objection phase of the sales process because he had rehearsed his responses to the objections, and he knew a deal was very close to closing after the first objection came up.

Training and role-playing with your team is crucial to handling objections. Some reps will literally just say "Okay" when they hear a no and move on to the next lead. Good training and modeling really helps bump the number in this area for sure.

I will then post these numbers across the board and allow my sales reps to train on each piece based on their numbers. For example, a high performer can be the sales manager for the day and train the others on his winning area. Good sales managers are always growing their people and training them to understand and be able to perform their jobs one day. Letting your stars teach your other reps is key to the overall development of your team.

What is the last piece of this puzzle? You guessed it— reengagement. How often do your reps contact clients after sales are closed? This number would be client contracts divided by clients. When you look at this number, you will realize that certain reps never call clients after the sale. The largest sales we get in our business come from existing clients; the fortune is in the follow-up. It takes time for a client to develop enough trust to make a purchase, and that initial purchase is often minimized to reduce the client's risk.

The second sale, however, will reinforce the first purchase based on the trust that has been established by the first sale. This is a ranked metric that when posted will point out some things about who is afraid to recontact their clients. More important, who needs training on this? Often your best closers. Some of them will think they got all the meat off the bone and calling again might equal a cancel. Those reps need to understand that they may have gotten all the fruit off the tree but more fruit will grow after the service has been properly provided, and that can be picked as well and perhaps by a competitor. Can you afford to feed your competition from your garden?

I learned that my reps with the most contracts per client called clients the day after the sale to reassure the clients and summarize the purchases. That connect built trust. The next calls would occur in seven days, one month, and every quarter till renewal time. The more interactions you have with a client, the more opportunity you have for an upsell. Many of the calls were just check-ins, but if clients answered or had new needs come up, the sales reps were all over that. Clients' needs change based on changes in their businesses, and you want your sales reps to be the first to know about these changes, not your competitors.

Develop an ideal contact protocol for your sales team to follow, and then compare all these numbers at your weekly meetings. Think about the last time you made a small first purchase and then went crazy. Anyone remember Columbia records? They'd get you going for pennies, and before you knew it, you'd given them hundreds of dollars because they'd gained your trust and shown you value. Once they had that, they knew they could ask for more. That company grew to over $1 billion just by asking for more from their existing clients. Now it's your turn. When should you recontact your clients after a sale?

To summarize, a sales manager's main role is to

1. identify what moves the needle for performance,
2. measure and communicate what moves the numbers to the team, and
3. strategize on ways to improve what matters.

When we identified the key metrics for USFCR sales process, we noticed the following (you need to find yours) metrics—leads/contacts, contacts/conversation, average proposal size, proposals/contracts, and contracts/clients. These numbers should be communicated daily or weekly depending on how important each one is. I like to track dials and proposals out daily and focus on these numbers constantly as they are the controllable ingredients of sales success.

We review the other numbers weekly. I like to email out the daily numbers and address the weekly numbers in the weekly meeting. You want to get the numbers out constantly because results improve where the focus goes, and that shows reps where they are on achievement of their sales targets. The more you communicate with your team, the less likely anyone will get off track. Analyze these numbers and you'll see how many dials and proposals are needed to hit your numbers, and the reps will be able to forecast their sales results based on these numbers.

The last role of the sales manager is to develop leaders in the team. Follow my model—allow other reps to give or run weekly meetings based on how well they did on certain metrics the previous week. You'll be developing future leaders. Leadership is showing your team that you have value by providing them with the data they need to chart their progress. Show them where they are, where they want to go, and what they need to do to get there; that's an essential role of a sales manager. By having daily and weekly items that you focus on, you'll be leading the team with the same steering device and keeping everyone on the same mission. The overarching job of a sales manager plain and simple is to make sure the team is all on the same page.

3.3 How to Coach Reps

*The interesting thing about coaching is that you have
to trouble the comfortable, and comfort the troubled.*
—Ric Charlesworth, Hockey

Coaching … I know a lot of you are thinking, *What's coaching got to do
with selling? This isn't sports.* But coaching is a term that's been used
in business management pretty aggressively for the last few years.
Coaching is leading someone without using strong demands. Coaching
in sales management is leading by asking questions. Coaches help the
members of their teams develop and sharpen their skills.

Sales managers and coaches are looking to establish a sense of
unity, combined responsibility, and they will continually use the word
we as in "We need to hit our numbers" rather than "You need to hit
your numbers." A good sales manager just like a good coach has the
team's best interests at heart. Good coaches will ask questions that
get the reps to find the answers they need and then want to change;
they don't simply demand performance.

Coaching is important because it's a way to quickly add skills
to your team by focusing on what each member needs and desires
coaching on. It also forces sales reps to take charge of their own
advancement. Good coaches ask empowering questions.

When you're coaching reps, you're getting them to take charge
of where they are and why they would want to change their
performance. Sales reps can have different goals, and coaches can
learn what those are, what motivates each of them. Once coaches
know their sales reps' motivators, they can keep those motivators in
front of them. Effective coaching will make the reps want to improve
their performance for their own reasons, not their coaches' or their
companies' reasons. Good coaches simply move their team forward.

I always wanted to serve the good sales managers I had, strong
relationships with. Have you had sales managers like that? Those
who asked you questions that made you want to perform better?
Coaches build strong, one-on-one relationships with their teams.
Coaching utilizes self-growth and personal interaction to form the
glue that builds and holds relationships together.

Being a great coach is easy; there are only a couple of steps to becoming one. The key is to make sure you remember to separate coaching and management. When you coach sales reps, make it all about what they want, not what you or your company wants. Coaching should be viewed as voluntary and a benefit to the employee. When I coach, I normally will be thanked by sales reps for spending time with them. Remember coaching is about finding out what the rep wants and moving that rep forward on that plan.

Here are steps to becoming an excellent coach.

1. Make sure it's about the sales reps first—their needs and goals.
2. Find out what motivates them.
3. Get their permission to coach; make sure they want to be coached.
4. Ask questions that get them thinking about what they want and how they can get there. These can be the same questions. Very rarely do we answer the same question the same way twice. (You'll learn more when you see the coaching questions below.)
5. Normalize any issues they're having. It's not the issues or the problems; it's what you do about them that matters. Ask, "What are you going to do to learn and grow from this obstacle?"
6. Leave the sales reps feeling happy and elevated with a focus on a compelling future.
7. Have a system to measure progress, celebrate the small wins, and hold the reps accountable.
8. Remember that after every problem comes another problem, so get your sales reps to understand problems are key to long-term growth.

The first two steps are easy. I know you really want to know what questions to ask. The questions should be simple; they should prompt thought and reflection. I give a couple sample questions below. You can ask the same questions over and over or create new ones depending on the issue. I prefer to do what works over and over, but if you want variety, you got it. My favorites are at the top by the way.

Coaching Questions

- What can I do to better help you?
- How could you learn and grow from this?
- Why do you really want to achieve what you want to achieve? What would achieving that really do for you?
- How could you work less but make more money?
- What do you love must about selling? How can we focus more on that?
- How can we have more fun at work?
- Why did you get in sales? Why are you still in sales?
- What things do I do that slow you down or complicate your work?
- What are the biggest challenges you have overcome this quarter? How did you do that?
- What could you do now to help you hit your quota next quarter?
- What could you do or change to increase your effectiveness in pursuing your goals?
- What is the single biggest threat to your making your sales quota? How can we fix that?
- What one thing do you know you need to change this month to get your sales numbers to improve?
- How could you fix the relationship with this or that person if you wanted to?
- What might make you consider fixing that relationship?
- What would happen if you did repair that relationship?

Questions like these will allow sales reps to think about how they can improve their performance. When someone tells you something, it's suspect, but when you speak it, it becomes a fact. Questions will provide the road map to hold sales reps accountable. Think about how much easier it is to motivate sales reps when you're using their maps. Often, sales managers tell reps to make more dials and they say they can't. However, if the sales manager asks, "What do you need to do to improve your performance?" the rep will often say, "I need to make more dials." Coaching such reps will allow you to uncover the real obstacles to their increasing their production and more important get them to see how they can break through and make the change.

Real change happens when it comes from inside, and coaching will allow your reps to go inside and find their own answers and more important the reasons they want to change. Everyone has the right answers inside; questions are the fishing hooks on your line to get them to the surface.

The last piece of coaching—and the most important—is to get sales reps focused on the future; get them to leave coaching sessions with a sense of what's possible. Coaching sessions are effective if they get reps to commit to upping their performance. They should leave the session with a desire to get back on the phone. They should feel that what they want is in their grasp and that they have an executable plan to follow.

If you have coaching sessions with each of your reps every two weeks, you'll develop massive closeness with your team that will likely translate to employee loyalty and increased output over time. As you get better at coaching, you can also do group coaching or mastermind coaching where you ask everyone questions and even do breakout sessions to share those answers with partners. Coaching is an essential tool to develop and maintain top talent, so make sure you make time to coach your reps.

How often do you plan on doing coaching with your team?

How will you make sure you split your coaching time between top- and bottom-tier performers? You can't spend all your time at the bottom and have a top-performing organization.

What are some key questions you will ask when you coach?

How can you keep your coaching calls on schedule and productive?

3.4 The Essentials—Gold Mining for Sales Management/Selling the Team on the Company

What is the one thing a sales manager can never forget? What makes a top performer? What is the mind-set of that performer? What are the essential ingredients to create top performers?

I've looked at the data and performed hundreds of interviews for sales positions and have learned that the top reason sales reps left a previous position was that they had lost faith in the product or service they were selling. Clients had beaten them down and left them disillusioned about what they were selling as I mentioned before. Good sales managers understand this phenomenon and counteract clients' negative words with positive words about the company and product.

No matter how great a company is, its sales reps will get beaten down by clients over time. Even Google gets client complaints. Just a few drops of chocolate syrup in milk will turn the glass dark. It's the same with your sales reps. It takes a proactive, constant, positive stream of good news such as new products being rolled out and success stories from happy clients to prevent sales reps' minds from turning dark.

In a normal sales organization, sales reps will get burned out over time. That's inevitable but normal. Most sales managers know that, but they elect to only treat burnout, not proactively prevent it. It's as if a doctor is saying, "Do whatever you want. I'll treat you with medicine later. The medicine might kill you, but come on—you were already dying when you came into the hospital, weren't you?" The best way to handle burnout is to make sure it doesn't happen in the first place.

Medicine in the sales environment does not always work well; many times, it's simply taking some time off: "You need a vacation." Many times, this medicine is given too late; when burned-out sales reps start looking for new jobs, it can be impossible to get them back on board with your team, and they can potentially taint the rest of your organization because negative thoughts and feelings spread quickly.

We can't quarantine our teams, so we need to be proactive, not reactive, when dealing with burnout. Give your team the constant vaccine of positive thoughts and keep burnout away.

Here are some stats on how often sales reps leave due to burnout.

- 44 percent of companies have programs to help employees who are burned out (Statista.com). All of these deal with the symptoms as well.
- Burnout causes a minimum 20 percent annual turnover in sales, and it's up to 34 percent if you include voluntary and involuntary turnover (Bridge Group).
- 71 percent of companies take six months or longer to onboard new sales reps; at a third of all companies, it takes nine months or more (Clear Slide and CSO Insights).

I wonder how many reps get burned out just during the onboarding period.

How much turnover in your organization is due to burnout?

I know the symptom is poor numbers, but was that the cause or effect of burnout?

How many reps do you have who are starting to get burned out?

<u>Here are some signs of burnout.</u>

- showing up late
- arguing about policy
- complaining about clients

- getting mad at order fulfillment
- being unhappy with the services the company offers
- saying they need a vacation
- complaining they have no time
- call reluctance

I could go on. The symptoms are everywhere, aren't they? Makes you see the value in keeping your team members positive, right?

Knowing that burnout is a predictable pattern much like winter, you need to prepare for it. On average, how many times will your sales reps be told no per day? How often do you resell your reps on how great your company is to work for and how great what they're selling is? How often do you shop the competition and find out all the stuff wrong with their offerings? When was the last time you had a client come in and do a video testimonial? Do you send out happy-client reviews weekly to your team? All of these things will help only if they are done consistently and well before burnout occurs, which can be irreversible if not treated. The effects of burnout often last for around three months after it is noticed.

Don't forget the negative effects of pre-burnout, which can yield reduced performance several months before burnout is even noticed. One burned-out sales rep can easily create a burned-out office. Deal quickly with the negativity and burnout in your office with a prevention plan. The coaching I mentioned in the previous chapter can really help to make sure you prevent burnout or at least catch it early. And no matter how much sales reps try to convince you they just need time off, vacations don't cure burnout. The only way to cure burnout long-term is to make sure your reps see their work as meaningful and valuable for themselves and their customers. If they love what they do, time disappears.

How can you get your sales team to love what they do again?

Goal Setting

It seems every book has a chapter on goal setting, so I know you're wondering if you should read this. I'm going to shed some light on goal setting and bring up some new topics I haven't seen elsewhere. It will be well worth your time.

As a sales manager, what is your responsibility with goal setting? Do you offer goal-setting advice on personal goals or just business goals? Long-term career path? What is it? What should you talk with a rep about when you're setting goals?

Let's start with an online article I found on salesreadinessgroup.com. Here are six common factors that motivate salespeople.

- money
- opportunity
- teamwork
- independence
- visibility
- excellence

These are six common factors; your reps will all have differences in their motivators, and uncovering them is the key to setting goals. They may also have different words they use to describe one of the six. With goal setting, you're trying to uncover and shine light on why a sales rep is working in sales.

Those motivated by money are normally easier to handle and normally do well with less management; they just need to know how much they can earn. The other five types are those you need to cultivate and work with to keep them focused. All salespeople will desire to have some of all of the above traits as well, but they will have their favorites, their carrots, and those will move them to their highest performance level.

Many reps don't work for money per se but the security it provides them and their families. Goal setting will be huge for them. Defining their achievable actions more in terms of how many clients they needs to bring aboard to buy bigger houses for their families rather than how much commission they will make will likely be a stronger motivator for them. Money dangled in front of them can actually scare them if they see it as representing time away from their family.

A sense of purpose is the true long-term driver of reps. The better you get at connecting the dots between what moves them individually and the mission of the organization, the more effective you will be at leading.

Many sales reps picked sales because it allowed them to work independently. Giving a rep like this additional latitude and freedom for selling a certain amount of deals may be a bigger motivator than the money for instance.

If you want to get more performance from you reps, you have to know what they want and then continually show them how their production is moving them toward that goal and especially if it's not money. If the goal is big enough and progress toward it is occurring, the energy and passion from the sales rep will shine out positivity to other team members and prevent burnout.

Here are some goal-setting questions.

- Are there any meaningful goals you want to achieve this year that could be affected by your performance at work?
- What would it look like when you achieve that goal?
- Who would it affect?
- How can I best help you maximize your time?
- How can I help you track and measure your performance?

3.5 How to Set Up Remote Sales Reps

Being a remote sales rep sounds like a great idea to sales reps, but the thought often terrifies sales managers. Managing something you can't see or touch may seem difficult on the surface, but it's actually not harder than managing an employee at the office; it's just very different.

Often, remote employees can be easier to manage but harder to motivate. However, remote reps won't create drama in the office and be the one bad apple there that spoils the bunch. It's easier to get remote reps to see the importance of hitting their numbers because brown-nosing and schmoozing is not very effective over the phone.

Leadership can be impossible with remote reps if a clearly defined system for performance and sales procedures isn't in place; the lack of one can easily erase the benefits of a remote sales staff. Leadership in a well-run organization is about much more than the leader; it's about a culture of leadership in the entire team. In a poorly run organization, leadership comes mainly from the directors, top-down.

I recommend setting up a buddy system for remote reps that allows strong reps or senior reps to lead and develop newer reps. The two will work together and form a relationship that allows the newer rep to gain knowledge and the seasoned rep to gain management experience or the ability to contribute to the team, whichever the rep prefers to call it. Pairing assets up allows for the magnification of the organization's purpose and leadership and creates a team environment, which is essential to getting long-term passion and involvement from the employee.

It's easy to get a remote-sales rep—put an ad out and hire one. You'll be able to attract good candidates when geography isn't a limiting factor. But you'll need a tested and scripted training system in place just as you would with any other system, one that includes partnering new remote reps with more-seasoned reps as I mentioned. You want strong targets for the new reps that are not dollar driven to make sure they work hard the first ninety days and not procrastinate. Have them check in somehow daily to make sure they're on the job.

Tracking activity-based numbers is essential to making sure your remote assets are really working. If you wait till the end of the pay period to look for results, you might have missed many days of inactivity. All reps will focus on what you manage, and what you manage will improve. Have junior reps submit activity reports to their senior reps. That will allow the senior reps to follow up on proposals the junior reps didn't close. Offer senior reps financial incentives to get the new reps to quickly meet their first sales quotas; that will significantly decrease the new reps' learning curve.

Remote reps are essential today. You might not let your entire staff work from home every day, but the trend of one or two days of working out of the house seems to be here to stay. I read a study that said by 2020, 50 percent of our workforce will be freelance contractors or remote workers—crazy to think about that. The internet is going to force us to allow our workforce more freedom, but currently, it is a great hiring and a strategic advantage for those companies smart enough to utilize it.

There's an opportunity of a lifetime available every day. You just have to find it, and remote sales is that opportunity right now. Get on the trend now while you can poach top talent from other organizations that are not willing to hire remote sales reps yet.

3.6 How to Develop Your Next Sales Manager

Developing your next sales manager is much more important than the actual work you do as a sales manager. To be a great leader, you need great leaders under you. Finding and training at least one potential replacement is key. We'll call these potential replacements your bench. A quote I say all the time is, "The success of a leader can be found in the strength of his bench."

Once you start to train your next sales manager, that allows you to

1. work less,
2. be more impactful,
3. quickly get your message out, and
4. be ready for promotion.

If you have no one to take over your current position, how could you move up? Have you ever known people who were stuck in their positions for years because no one wanted or was qualified to take their jobs? Having no legacy plan is the sign of a dead-end job for the manager and his or her reports. For your next opportunity to open up, you have to delete your current opportunity.

To develop your next sales manager, sell your prospect on the benefits of being a sales manager. Often, sales reps may not be committed to their current roles let alone to hanging around for several years to get a promotion. Get on the same page with the sales rep to find out what his long-term motivators are and then align that with the company and his current role. Think of a time when you did something that was clearly work but was fun. What were you doing? What made it fun? Could you add that one thing to another task to make that task fun? When we ask these questions, we start to realize that certain things make life fun and that it's not the task but often its components we focus on that makes the task fun. Volunteering with a bunch of great people and making a difference can be fun even if that requires being in the hot sun for twelve hours. Think about how you can align the fun parts of the job with the sales reps' motivators to first get the rep really aligned with and passionate about his current role.

After the sales rep is fully aligned and committed, you can start to sell the benefits of being a manager. You will want to align these benefits with his motivators. For example, if the rep really likes having freedom, you can explain how he gets the freedom to structure his day and help the rep be productive and have some daily freedom. If the rep really wants to make money, you can explain that the sales manager's job has a much larger base and offers many opportunities to make a lot more money down the line. If the sales rep wants to spend more time with his family, you can tie in the fact that he'll have the flexibility to spend time with his family as well as create a great work family he manages as well.

Getting reps sold on their current positions and growth is one of the main jobs of a sales manager. Often, employees will feel there's no growth in their current positions. Get your team to see that advancement opportunities are based on how they do, not how long they've been doing it. Getting all those on your team to want a promotion for instance will get them to show up in a way that will give them a higher likelihood of being promoted and allowing the company to grow and create more opportunities for that promotion.

Sales reps who want to be promoted will take on extra tasks; this new ambition will help out with both sales management and leadership. I often have reps who are being groomed for management coach underperforming reps. These successful reps are often the best teachers and motivators for new team members as well. A sales manager who is not closing deals every day will not be anywhere near as effective at teaching and motivating a sales rep as will a superstar who wants to help. The key for sales managers is to get all on their teams to want to help their teams. The foundation for that motivation is getting them all to want to advance in the company.

Once you achieve that, it's time to put together the metric for how to select the one you'll promote. You'll want to promote this metric and have your key prospects understand and focus on it daily. When I think of the metrics that matter most for promotion, I consider my current key performance indicators that demonstrate I'm performing at a high level. Once you have a good answer to these questions, you can break down the top three metrics and let the sales reps know these are the three most important things for them to focus on.

Here are the top three metrics for my company.

1. Likeability of team, having a respect and love for its members
2. Demonstrating ability to go above and beyond without being asked or looking for financial reward; doing it solely to help the team
3. Strong ability to communicate

I know my goals are vague; I'm with you there. But these are how I tell whom to promote. I will very often promote someone who based on a spreadsheet looks like a poor move, but through my metrics and study, I'm able to spot the right candidate who would be missed on a spreadsheet.

By communicating these goals to the team in advance, they will often understand and appreciate the member who got the promotion and consider it a fair and ethical decision. So many companies wait till they need someone before they start looking for a replacement. The time to look is now so you'll have time to build and develop your replacement.

Last, make sure you're ready to be promoted. Ask your superiors, "What do you need to see to promote me? What would the likely timeline be for this promotion?" Communicating that you're looking to move up or around in the organization is key to allowing this to happen. Anyone who works at a company and more specifically at the same position there for more than three years will have a high likelihood of becoming bored and unmotivated. Movement is key, so look to move before you become burned out and bored. It can take years to demonstrate the abilities necessary to move up to many senior-level management positions, but you can start demonstrating your abilities the first day you start on the job.

If you work for yourself, this can often be harder to do and is the main reason small firms have trouble attracting and keeping top talent. A firm can grow only if its owner is willing to truly hand off responsibilities to his team. A company will have nothing to offer its top performers if the owner isn't ready to allow his team to take over his current duties.

When you are communicating to your team as an owner, your goal should be to get the company running with zero dependence on you. You should be able to say, "If I get hit by a bus tomorrow, nothing will happen to my company. I want to purely be an added value to the organization." Having an exit plan for your ownership interest in case something happens to you as the business owner is also one of your responsibilities. The more planning you do to remove yourself from the day-to-day work of the company, the larger it company can grow.

In review, the most important things you can do as a sales manager is to get your team sold on working at your company, selling the products of the company, and moving up in the company. The clearer you can be on how to move up in the company, the more opportunity for growth the sales reps will see. Even if you have only one position for management in your small company, there's no reason not to train reps for promotion because you may expand for example. If your employees want to advance but have nowhere to go in your company or are not gaining skills, they'll leave.

Love your team, develop your team, and develop yourself, not one without the others, is the secret to management success.

3.7 How to Increase a Price

You can determine the strength of a business over time by the amount of agony they go through in raising prices.

—Warren Buffett

In periods of inflation, price increases can become necessary. Many times, sales reps will think that a price increase means the product will be harder to sell, but that is a limiting belief; overcoming that is what we'll focus on in this chapter.

Sales reps can be very defensive when anyone changes their commission structure or the price of the product they're selling. This defensive reaction is natural and to be expected. As a sales manager, your job is to make sure you frame the price increase as a blessing and a short-term setback. Acknowledging the short-term issue is key to disarming the sales reps. If you fail to recognize that there are some issues with the price increase, you will give the sales reps the ammo they need to lash out against you. Get them together and say, "We have some issues. If we strategize together I think we can easily get through them. I'll then explain the price increase and ask for everyone's feedback."

During such sessions, I expect to get some negative responses. When I do, I turn the conversation from the negatives and spend at least four times more time talking about how we could frame the price increase to our clients in a way that would make it a benefit for them and us. After doing that, I go over why we have price increases, why it's necessary to raise the price of products, and how price increases help our clients. Getting your team to focus on coming up with a solution for a price increase will often yield better results than anything you could do independently because the team will likely come up with great ways to get this spun in a way that makes more sense to clients. Never be scared to ask your team for help. We all love challenges as they make life interesting and fun, but we all hate being told what to think or do; we want to be involved. So involve your team; let your team be in on the solution.

When such a meeting is wrapping up, I go again through the reasons we need to raise prices.

1. We need to maintain our position in the market. If we are best of breed, price is often what sets us off.
2. We need to be able to invest in new products and key people to allow the company to innovate and be around for the long term.
3. Investing in marketing has costs, and though you have a higher priced product, increased branding will command a higher price.
4. What has not gone up? I mean, everything that's worth buying goes up in price. Everything feels bad only because it's different.
5. If we don't raise prices at all over the next five years, we'd surely be out of business. Let's move forward and focus on what we can control.

3.8 How to Deliver a Sales Meeting

> Sales are contingent upon the attitude of the salesman, not the attitude of the prospect.
> —William Clement Stone

A sales manager's main role is to deliver sales meetings. Sales meetings have different expectations based on whom you ask.

In your opinion, what makes a good sales meeting? What are the items that really set a meeting off as worth your time and make it impactful?

It's always good to think about the feelings, emotions, and action you want your team to perform before you design your meeting. Often, sales meetings in which reps are scolded for whatever reason don't address the bigger issue of what state of mind and readiness sales managers want the reps to leave the meeting with. Scolding doesn't result in better performance. Sales meetings should focus on how to fix an issue, not just demonstrate that the sales manager is observant. Being observant in finding faults is often the most dangerous action a sales manager can take. When we're fault finding, we often make assumptions, and that violates the first rule of life: never assume anything and especially concerning people.

I've conducted thousands of sales meetings. I normally do at least three per week, and I've found that when they're done correctly, my team will look forward to them. The key to doing them correctly is keeping them on time and making sure to address the items the sales reps desire. Most sales reps for instance are always interested in hearing and learning new ways to increase their sales and especially ideas of how to work less and make more. New sales techniques or more specifically examples of new techniques can work extremely well.

I make sure everyone has a voice by having brainstorming and sharing sessions. I like to use my meetings as ways to start a discussion that everyone gets involved in on topics I know will meet my outcomes for the meeting. I always make sure my meetings no matter how good they are end on time. I let my sales reps know how much I value their time and appreciate their coming to them and participating in them. I've been to many bad meetings that dragged on; I've learned the key is to always end on time.

We have three meetings a week so we can always carry a meeting into the next week. Such carryover to the next meeting makes reps more excited about attending the next meeting. I'll also target who attends my meetings; new reps go to all three while senior staff may attend only one. I also have special meetings with team members who need additional training or are having issues.

Here are the key outcomes and points I put into my meetings.

1. Focus on how great the company is doing.
2. How lucky I feel to work with such a great team.
3. What's coming up (very important).
4. Example of a previous rep's success.
5. Example of a happy client (testimonial).
6. Teach or reinforce a sales skill.
7. Get the reps excited to go back out and sell.
8. Focus the reps on what's possible at this organization—highest outcome of job
9. Pulling the team together.
10. Getting everyone on the same page (this really can never be completed, only reinforced).

When you make a list and set your meetings up to focus on key outcomes, it will make them flow better and have more impact. Without getting your brain to visualize how the meeting will end and what the reps will take away, you'll rarely get the key outcomes you want. Leaving a meeting up to luck will result in a meeting that drags on and gets nothing done. At any meeting, your reps will all be asking themselves, *Is this a waste of my time?* Be sure to respect their time; end the meeting early if possible, and structure them to make sure the reps get the most value possible out of the meeting.

Think about the last horrible sales meeting you attended. What happened? What advice would you give your old sales manager if you could? Now think of a meeting that went well. What made that meeting go well?

Now that I have you thinking about what a bad meeting looked like as well as what a good meeting looked like, you're ready to see the meeting flow I use.

Meeting Flow—Think Interaction

1. Set the agenda; be respectful of everyone's time. (This shows you did some planning.)
2. Ask a question to start getting everyone engaged. This can also be a raise your hand if … or a Who did this or that? I try to quickly get everyone involved.
3. Go over some facts—numbers, a handout—something concrete. (Visuals are a must here.)
4. Ask for input or feedback from the team, show you value them and need their help on an issue or just even the current meeting setup.
5. Recap meeting. (The most important part.)
6. Sell the next meeting and agenda; you want your team to not want to miss a meeting.

I have Monday and Friday morning meetings for my entire team. I have a meeting on Wednesdays for new reps and those who are struggling. This smaller meeting allows me to learn about each new rep and hold mini mastermind groups that let each of my team members help handle the other team members' issues and problems. These small mastermind groups are also a way for me to develop and spot future managers.

Remember that your next leader might not be your top salesperson. The best players on the bench are those who follow the rules well, meet your performance expectations, are liked by the team, and are willing to go above and beyond.

If you are new to meetings and are having trouble getting your team to be excited to attend, add more interaction. No matter how good a speaker you are, if you talk for thirty minutes straight, you'll likely lose your audience. Plan thirty-minute meetings but get interaction from the attendees every three to seven minutes. From time to time, I'll play a YouTube video first and ask for feedback from everyone about the sales or motivational strategy used. That's a great way to get everyone ready for the meeting.

3.9 How to Develop a High-Performance Culture on Your Sales Team

> Nothing can stop the man with the right mental attitude from achieving his goal; nothing on earth can help the man with the wrong mental attitude.
> —Thomas Jefferson

When thinking about high performance, the first thing most people think about is results. Performance is measurable; it's defined by how well someone does compared to a benchmark. It's important to understand what the performance goals for your team are, but it's more important to understand the building blocks of that performance. High-performing reps went through certain steps or phases of performance before they became superstars.

Common Four Building Blocks of Sales

1. new business
2. renewal
3. upsells
4. former client win backs

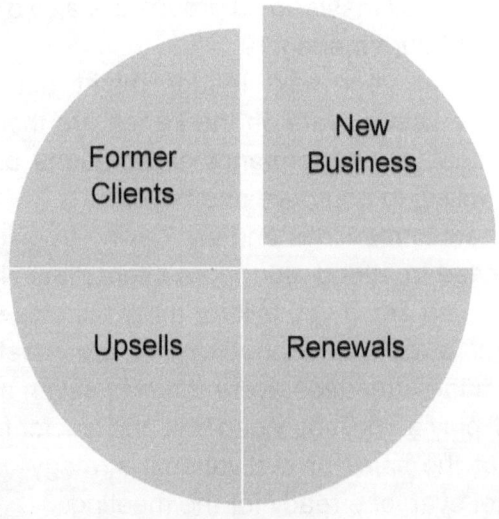

What is the average value for each of these sales in your organization? What percentage of sales do your top performers get from each of these segments? How could you build a map for your sales reps to get to $200k using each of these four movers of income? You might tell a rep, "You need fifty renewals, twenty new clients, twenty upsells, and twenty former clients to sign up to make $200k this year. Last year, you made $135k, and the only difference was the ten upsells and ten former client win backs. I know you've never called your former clients, so I think this is a great opportunity for you especially with the new pricing we're offering to former clients who come back." Are you starting to see how to use this? Great! Stay with me; this is about to get good.

A good sales manager is a detective who's good at finding out how high performance occurs, the steps that lead to it—the mile markers, the reward points (or what they should have been). The first thing reps need to do to achieve high performance is to develop the mind-set of a high performer and desire to become one themselves. What can cause that? Everyone's different, but getting reps to tap into the reason they would step away from the pack and perform at a higher level is key. That will create urgency in them to move in that direction. Remember that hunger is the highest human motivator.

Once you have your reps identifying with their reasons to increase their performance are, make performance reachable and reward the effort it takes them to reach it. Great managers understand that confidence is built off prior success; sometimes, they have to create confidence by rewarding a rep a little before it's completely deserved. If reps have a goal of getting $15,000 in sales for the week and the first week they get $4,500, you could reward them by letting them know that was a great performance for the first week on the job. You can also compare the current performance to the previous week's performance and acknowledge the growth of reps' individual performances week over week.

For reps to move from selling $0 to $15,000, they will have to hit milestones. Your job as a sales manager is to identify those milestones and clearly communicate a timetable for reaching them. Make the first few attainable or they'll get discouraged way too early; that won't create a high-performance mind-set. Their confidence will grow, and you can establish tougher milestones to reach after that.

When I managed, I would often sit with new reps and even help them get their first sales in a way that I could give them all the credit. If you want to teach a man to fish, you have to make sure he feels he can fish. And the quickest way to get him to feel confident he can fish is to reward him for catching a fish even if he didn't land it all on his own. Reward him for doing the key components of catching the fish. In the same way, show reps that they are ahead of where they started; that will start to build their confidence.

After their confidence level is higher and they're achieving the outcomes set for them, tell them what it means for the organization as a whole. Great managers get new sales reps to feel appreciated and valuable well before they look for a return on the hire. Trying to squeeze juice from a fruit before it's ripe wastes energy. Laying a strong foundation of appreciation and growth by allowing new rep to hit obtainable targets will ensure that they survive and produce fruit. As a leader and manager, you can set the standards of performance for each segment of your team members. The more mile markers of performance you establish, the more times you'll have to show your appreciation when your reps meet them. Each time you show appreciation to your sales reps for high performance, you build high performance in your team.

When I first started managing reps, I had the mind-set that people could either sell or not sell. I know you've likely had this mind-set or may even still have it. The rationale behind the statement is correct, but as a sales manager, your question should be why that is the case. Finding the answer to this million-dollar question could instill high performance on your team. Superstar reps you hire from another organization will have a high level of confidence and will quickly advance in your organization whereas new reps who were just fired for poor performance at another organization will struggle. Having a system set up to reward performance early on will allow your high performers to ramp-up quickly and your average performers to start the journeys to high performance.

It's normal for new reps to have trouble learning a new process when they're not confident in themselves. If you're having issues with your sales team learning processes and keeping up with procedures, that's often linked to an environment where performance is underrecognized and confidence is weak. In such an environment, your underperforming members will start asking themselves, *Why can't I get this? This is over my head. I need to find something easier. This is way too complex for me.* When you sense that, look at reducing the difficulty of short-term targets and increasing rewards for your team for hitting smaller targets. Remember to promote the high-performance belief in your team.

After you have set up a good onboarding program that clearly outlines performance and has multiple points to reward it, you can start to get some bottom-line performance for the organization. It's then time to start looking to squeeze juice from the fruits of your labor. The longer you wait to start juicing the fruit the better. If you have a really good environment, the team will literally juice the fruit for you—they won't need to see management's stick because they're focused on the carrot.

Different people will respond to things differently; not everyone will want to chase the highest mountain. To get all your team to high performance, you need to establish performance markers for rewards and standards for minimum levels of performance. Reps who achieve over the minimum level of performance are providing value to the organization; those who aren't need a tailored plan for improvement. The clearer you can make the expectations of maximum and minimum performance, the more likely you are to get positive revenue performance from your team.

So now that we have set up the carrot and the stick, how do we get the team to want to become top performers? This comes down to conditioning and recognition of performance again. Reps tend to always rank themselves internally and highlight a few individuals as high performers. Those not in the top portion of the pack will often feel they're low performers. Some will even blame the system or claim favorites are being played. Usually, if your team rates performance only internally, you'll have only a few A players and everyone else will feel inferior to them, and that can erode a high-performance mind-set quickly. There's an easy answer to this I wish I had known about when I started managing. This is worth a few million dollars—do not relate performance only internally. If I have ten reps, I'd have three stars, four average players, and three duds. The duds would need a lot of coaching to move up on the board a little, but in all reality, they'll never be stars because we most likely have conditioned a low performance belief in them that has become part of their identity. If I instead set up a new form of monitoring performance that stacks up on a wider ranking system, I'll change the game and have an environment in which everyone is a high performer since we are not just looking internally for rank.

Tell your team members that you consider them high performers if they sell ten widget a week; it doesn't matter where they rank in the team. Sounds genius, right? Think about how hard it can be for someone to be at the bottom of the board for years. Ask yourself now why the board needs a bottom. Everyone who sells ten widgets a week is a star. Stay with me. This will get interesting.

I know you're saying, "That sound great, Dan, but how can I do that?" I've done this simply by creating performance standards for good sales reps based on external performance metrics. For example, you could google how much annual revenue was closed, lead closing percentages, and the number of proposals submitted per week for average sales reps in your industry, not your company—think broadly. You could then calculate performance based on those numbers and show a high-performance standard that was not only internal. If you have competitors that are publicly traded, you can look through their financials and find out what their average sales rep generates in revenue. Having a classification system for your reps based on external, not just internal, metrics will allow you to potentially have all high performers on your team. If you fail to do this, you'll always be staring at an internal bell curve of performance. You'll always be looking for another superstar only to realize that that superstar might effectively kick out one of your current superstars. This will also move top performers to perform better.

If you have a new organization, your sales may be well off the national level for instance. Showing your top performers what's possible in an external organization will give them a new frame of reference and targets to go after that will increase their performance and allow your other team members to move up as well.

Your goal as a sales manager is to find a way of labeling all your sales reps as top performers. This label needs to be based on solid mile markers and should be conditioned with your sales reps. I always cringe when I ask sales managers to tell me about their teams and they say, "I have stars, a bunch of steady old timers, and a few I need to get rid of." They then ask me how to fix the reps. It's not the reps who needs fixing; it's the labels we're putting on the reps that needs fixing if we want to change.

What could stop all this high-performance stuff from working? You guessed it—the reps' own attitudes: "I'm average." "I can't sell like the others can." "My family prevents me from selling as much as I can." "My health is too bad to be a high performer." "Those are reps have no ethics." Great leaders uncover these attitudes in their reps and find ways to get them on the high-performance train. Conditioning of high performance with enough repetition will transform even the least confident to stardom. Even if they've been suffering from such negative conditioning for years, it can be removed and they can become high performers.

Find out how to set up targets easier to hit for your more complicated cases. You can reward based on growth from the previous week, year, and so on. Find the numbers that are improving and stress that they're getting better daily. High performance is not an accident; it's a conditioned mind-set the team can adopt based on the direction and support of its leader.

3.10 What to Measure—Proposals

The concept of what to measure from a sales manager's perspective seems so obvious, but so many managers make fatal mistakes by measuring the wrong items—the uncontrollables. When you're managing a sales team, maintaining a high-performance environment is crucial to your success. The key items measured in the organization are the main drivers of what creates a high-performance environment and culture.

You as a sales manager might measure only how much revenue is generated by your team, but is sales revenue really a controllable number? Can reps really determine how much money they'll earn any one day? And what would happen if your clients started thinking your sales reps were purely hunting for cash? The main thing to look for when you're deciding what to measure is what changes in controllable factors can contribute to building a high-performance culture.

I know, you're thinking, *How will I hit my sales numbers if I don't have my team focused on revenue? Aren't sales reps only dollar-motivated anyway?* Those are valid questions, but we want to look at what the components that make up the dollar are and get those components down to the controllable parts that make up the whole. If I want to get $20,000 in sales from each of my reps in a week, should I tell them that, or should I frame it in terms of what that would mean for them in commissions? I'd have a much better chance to connect with them if I told them, "I want you all to be on pace to make at least $250,000 this year. I know you have the ability, so I want us to come up with a strategy to do that." Once you have their attention, you can ask each one, "Where do you make most of your sales? What controllable action yields the most return for you?" Once you have the answers to these items from the reps, you can start to find out what would be a good item to track from your team.

Over the last fifteen years, I have learned that there are some constants when it comes to what items to measure; they are consistent across all the organizations I've worked with. Stay with me. The most important item to track is proposals; however, many reps hate to put out proposals. They almost get insulted when they spend fifteen minutes typing one out that doesn't close. This shift needs to change in your organization. Many types of buyers will not buy if they don't see it in writing, and larger organizations will have multiple decision makers; proposal are the only way to get buy-in and allow your deal to close. Your reps should view proposals as the main controllable outcome of their day. The more proposals submitted, the more business your team can close. Proposal equal pipeline, which equals larger paychecks.

To fully wrap your head around proposals for your team, calculate the value of each proposal your sales reps send out. That will be the most important metric you can record for your team. This number is proposals sent out divided by the number of signed contracts.

The next statistic I want you to measure is the average commission on closed deals—the number of a rep's sales (for at least a month) divided by the total sales commission paid to the rep. With these two numbers, you can effectively manage your entire sales organization.

When you're setting your targets, if they are revenue-wide numbers as most are, take the average revenue per contract to base your team's targets on. I'll talk more about this in a minute; I just want to get you thinking here. I'll show you a few more ways to move you into advanced territory, but this is the simplest piece and the one you want to focus on.

If I know my reps close one out of every two proposals they submit and the average commission they receive per client is $1,000, how many proposals does my sale rep have to submit each week to be on track to make $100k per year? The answer is about four, two of which they will close and earn $2,000 per week on. That means the dollar value per proposal is $500. Show the math to your reps and watch the lightbulbs go off in their heads about the value of sending out proposals. That's happened with my reps when I crunched these numbers for them. They saw that proposals were levers they could pull daily, levers they had control over, levers that could help them reach their milestones.

Sales reps are under tremendous pressure every day to perform, and tying that performance to a controllable aspect of their job is key. Sales reps burn out because they have negative feelings about work that keep them from performing and advancing in their careers. For some reps, going as little as one week without a sale will do that to them, and it can take weeks to take a rep from being burned out to being productive. Using this model of tracking and rewarding proposals being sent out will allow reps to realize that doing so will pay off, that commissions are coming.

Now that we have proposals as our measuring stick, we can set targets for each rep for how many proposals he or she sends out each day. You won't be asking for sales; you'll be asking for proposals out. That shift in focus will make your team much more productive and sincere when it comes to client interaction. The reps will not view their clients as only paychecks. I've seen immediate shifts in happiness and morale in reps we moved from a dollar-tracking system to a proposal-tracking system, or more simply put, an activity-based system.

Now onto more-advanced numbers and metrics you can roll out as your team masters the first couple of concepts. The first one is average dollar value of submitted proposals. As we get more granular, we will want to know the close ratio and the average size of proposal submitted in relation to the average size of deal closed. This number will tell you a lot about what kinds of deals your reps are proposing. You can also look at what's closing and find out if they're submitting giant proposals but closing only the smaller ones for example. You can use this formula to assess weaknesses in their presentation models. Remember the two components that make up success—the average size of order and the quantity of those orders broken down to the reps' average value per proposal. The more you can track, reward, and measure proposals out, the easier it will be to create and maintain a high-performance culture in your organization.

I told you I would give you some bonus material; just don't roll this out to your team until they're fully tracking and reporting and understand the value of proposals. To track the proposal number, have your team report the number of proposals submitted every day to you. Divide that by the number of closed sales and come up with the average commission sales generated as I mentioned earlier to get the average value per proposal, the most valuable number.

Some reps will not want to track the numbers saying it will slow them down, so you need to frame it in a way that will speed them up. It can take time to get everyone on board, but a contest or even some simple recognition can be a good way to do that.

To find out the next components worth tracking, we need to look at what makes up proposals. Proposals are made up of hours worked, dials, emails, appointments, appointments kept, and presentations. As a sales leader, you can dive deeper and start to track how these numbers play into the equation or at least explain them to your team.

When you look at the flow from a dial to a closed contract, you will notice many fallout points in the process. The more data you can track, the easier it will be to diagnose where your reps may have holes in their presentations. If you have a rep who has ten appointments per day but only one person shows each day for an appointment, the rep should work on doing a better job of reminding clients about the appointments or even setting the appointment up sooner—tomorrow, not next month. If certain reps are having a ton of conversations but no proposals, you might want to record and go over with them some of their calls or role-play with them.

Sales management is all about measuring the right information that leads to high performance, focusing your team on the controllables, and showing appreciation for the hard work they do daily. If your team aims for daily targets they can hit, that will build confidence and performance daily. This model will push average players to want to become above average and allow them to feel satisfied and rewarded for putting in a hard day's work.

3.11 How to Reinforce Processes and Procedures

I have a very strict gun control policy: if there's a gun around, I want to be in control of it.

—Clint Eastwood

You've heard clients say, "No one told me that!" That's also one of the worst things sales managers can hear from their reps. Employees have learned that this excuse normally works for everything, so it can be hard to tell if it's true or just a conditioned response. No one likes to be punished or look inferior, so they'll come up with excuses when they make mistakes.

Sales reps in particular can be masters at pushing the blame for mistakes off on their managers. Normally, at least it means you have persuasive salespeople working for you. But managers on top of their game can quickly tell if this is a valid excuse by referring to a simple procedure when rolling out information and content that I call the rule of eight. You need to reinforce at least eight times each new item you're rolling out to your team before you can expect it to be followed. I already can hear your objection—"Eight times?" I know, it sounds like a lot, but there are very easy ways to do this, and it will get your team on the same page, and that's priceless. Because people rarely write down anything anymore, you need to really burn your message into their brains. Less content plus repetition equals more; that's the formula for education.

A good leader understands the importance of getting everyone to understand and follow procedures. Teams on which one or two are missing information can cause tremendous confusion and chaos across an organization. Solving the problem of getting information quickly rolled out across teams was how I invented the rule of eight. I learned this from listening and studying great speeches and especially Martin Luther King's "I have a dream" speech; he repeated that phrase eight times in a context that allowed everyone who heard it to remember it. In that famous Disney song, the words

"It's a small world" are repeated forty-three times. No wonder kids remember that.

Repetition is one of the key components of memorization. Another one is the excitement or emotion surrounding the message. Kids who visit Disney World get excited and remember the event vividly for years. So when your reps are half asleep at your morning sales meeting, you might need a tad more repetition. Especially if you want the message to be lasting.

What's the best way to repeat your message? Have a written handout in physical form and online that contains all the key items you want to hold your sales reps accountable for. It provides the foundation for their following your rules. Reps won't tell you they didn't get something if you hand it to them and tell them it's also online; they'll have no excuses true or not true. They'll know exactly what they're responsible for. You'll still have to help reps understand the content, but you'll always be able to direct them to the publicly posted rules. They'll do so before they ask you a question.

Online posts and handouts are great, but you then have to make sure your team understands their content. When I use the rule of eight when reinforcing content, I

1. verbally explain the information,
2. distribute the handouts,
3. mention where it is on line,
4. give a story or example of how the rule will work,
5. explain the benefit the content has for the rep,
6. give an example of doing the action ineffectively,
7. ask what the rule means to the team and get clarity on that, and
8. recap the content.

In five minutes, I can do all eight things. I may have to bring this same message up at the next meeting depending on how everyone grasped the information previously, but I normally recap the last meeting since it's normal for 10 percent of my sales team to be out on any given day. Today's alarm clocks just aren't as reliable as they used to be.

When you are reinforcing key items with your team, remember

that everyone learns differently. Develop a strategy to go over key items with those on your team who can miss items; do this maybe one on one, or ask if anyone needs clarification on anything. You could also ask them to clarify what the rule or change means to them to make sure they're on the same page with you. Great leaders know how to communicate with each person on their teams and establish an environment in which they feel they can handle changes and updates.

Using repetition and different ways to present information using the rule of eight will help make sure your team is not overwhelmed and is following your instructions. I had one teammate who would take weeks to understand things; he kept asking everyone other than me how to do things. I quickly realized I wasn't teaching him in a way he could understand, so I would have some one-on-one meetings with him before I'd roll it out to others and ask him to write down an easy way for me to explain this to the team. His writing it down and thinking how to explain it to the team drove the information deeper into his brain, and he remembered it. Also, my using his input for the team gave him confidence that he could understand it. He ended up being one of my best and most loyal assets once I figured out a better way to communicate with him.

3.12 How to Share Success Stories

> Your success story is a bigger story than whatever you're trying to say on stage. Success makes life easier. It doesn't make living easier.
>
> —Bruce Springsteen

Sharing success stories may be the single biggest preventer of burnout in your team. **When you look at what burns reps out, you'll find it's due to negative feelings about work.** To understand burnout, you have to understand what work is—doing things without purpose. That feeling causes burnout, so focus on giving your reps a sense of purpose; they need to understand why they are doing what they are doing, and success stories can show them that. Success stories can connect the dots between the service, the reps' sales, and the value the clients receive. That's essential to maintaining a positive workforce.

I like to get and share as many success stories as I can. The best ways to capture success stories are with video, audio, email, social media, and review websites. I have found that sales reps are horrible at getting reviews and capturing success stories. My production department is normally the best at getting this data. I have set up a simple email that we send out requesting reviews to all clients. We personally thank those who respond or give a review. We try to get either a better email example or set up a phone call to learn more and possibly get a video or an audio testimonial that we can combine with other marketing material.

I share testimonials with my team after I have personally spoken with the clients who gave them. That way, I can add more light and make the success story seem more real. I can also help steer the clients to give added information to make it more relevant to the team.

So many businesses use their success stories but only externally. I use ours internally so my team learns they're doing good and making a difference in the community. Reps who feel they're making a difference will make sales numbers skyrocket on their own. Clients can feel the energy of sales reps who believe in their products. Your goal as a sales manager is to make sure your team members believe in your product, and success stories are the best way to get them to believe in it.

At my company, I tried to get at least ten reviews or good words and send them out on Wednesdays to our entire team; that way, more than just the sales team knew about them. I'd then in Monday meetings thank all the reps whose clients sent in positive reviews. I would then highlight a specific client review based on the product purchased and highlight several things that were relevant that also needed to be addressed that week as I was going over the review.

Getting your reps to see the benefits of the solution you're selling helps make sure they constantly focus on their clients and what happens when the solution works, not just on what happens if it doesn't work. Reviews are also a great way to maintain morale and reinforce the purpose behind the work they do.

3.13 Role-Playing

Role-playing is definitely one of the best ways to reinforce any sales process information. Reps can never get too good at handling objections, closes, or opens of sales presentations. Role-playing embeds a concept in your nervous system so that it's ready for you whenever you need it. I can memorize a script for example, but if I'm put on the spot with a client, I'll go to my default setting, and that default setting is what you have role-played consistently.

If your reps have never role-played, their default setting will likely be either an endless-loop conversation or some form of telling clients what they should do. Either one of these natural responses will produce far different results than a well role-played sales process will.

Role-playing questions with your team is more important than role-playing long scripts. A good question I like to role-play is, if you were to consider using a firm like ours, what would be the key reasons?

Whenever I talk about scripts and role-playing, I normally get a lot of resistance from sales reps and managers alike: "We have a high-end product, and our clients are too sophisticated for a script." I normally respond with a question: "Do your high-end clients have time to waste when they're looking at your company? Is sales all luck, or is there some science to it? Are their certain objections you hear every day? Could you practice and get better at handling those objections?"

The more you analyze the key points in the sales process and focus your role-playing on these parts, the better your team will get. We'd frequently hear, "I can't afford that," and before we role-played, our reps would normally start an argument with the client over a product's affordability. In role-playing, we trained reps to agree with clients who gave that objection and say, "Most business owners we work with can't afford to pay outright for the service either, but if you were to purchase the program despite the cost, what might be the reasons you decided to move forward?"

Role-playing also only works when it's overdone. When I say overdone, I mean done to the point that it's just ringing in your head like that "It's a small world" jingle. When I did sales at my first sales job selling cars, we would role-play every day at our company meeting. Role-playing every day was repetitive, but it got us to warm up on each other instead of on the customers. A professional athlete will warm up for hours before a game, so doesn't it seem logical that a sales rep would role-play for five to ten minutes to get ready to talk with a client? Having a drill and set system for role-playing is key. I like to do it first thing in the morning. Once your team does it for a few weeks, they'll start to like the social aspect of it and realize that it really increases their energy. After a good role-playing session, your team should want to get on the phone and sell something.

Have your team help you create a role-playing program, and let their input increase their buy-in of the program. You need their help and buy-in to get them to participate at a high level during your role-playing sessions.

To build out a good role-playing program, set up buddies; pair people for key reasons. Assign a new rep as the teammate of someone on track to become a manager. Assign those who are on their way out or performing poorly to each other, not new reps. Your superstars need to be paired with other superstars. They'll see very little benefit in working with low performers unless they want to become managers. I let my top performers choose their own partners in recognition of their performance. Superstars who see value in role-playing will prompt others to see the value as well.

After that, role-play for five to ten minutes on the different parts of the sales process progressing through each—opening the lead, setting up appointments, covering key questions, presentations, closes, objections, referral gathering, following up, and upselling. They should role-play until it's like a script they've committed to memory that will come up instinctually, automatically.

I focus an entire week on each part and drill the same content over and over so that it becomes ingrained. Role-playing is effective only when it uses intense repetition and is fun. Your team should know the why behind role-playing and want to be a part of it.

Keep it simple. I will often role-play the entire time around one sentence because most reps can't remember an entire paragraph after a couple of days, but a well-rehearsed sentence or two can become automatic.

Role-playing is one of the most effective ways to get your team to learn and then implement effective sales processes. It prevents your team from warming up on customers, and often the customers they warm up on are your best customers. What leads normally get called first? Your best leads. How much better would you be with power lifting if you warmed up first?

Role-playing is effective only if it's structured and utilizes effective repetition to make sure the content is always ready on demand. In sales, if you need to think about something, you're in trouble. Sales scripts need to be rehearsed so many times that they become automatic. Think how easy it is to drive home from work. Sales should be the same. We need to get out of the nonworking habits and condition the ones that work with role-playing.

When I worked at Verizon, mystery shoppers would test our sales team's ability to follow the sales process. Only the sales managers who did role-playing with their teams passed by having all their teams follow the sales process. Verizon spent eight weeks in training sales reps, but the reps would forget all their training within six months because it wasn't conditioned daily. Arnold Schwarzenegger said that if something's worth doing, it's worth doing daily. Role-playing is worth doing, so do it daily.

3.14 How to Fire Someone

I've never enjoyed firing anyone even when I hated being around that person. Go ahead and call me a softie. But there's an art to firing someone. Until I learned that art, I had the worst experiences with firing sales reps. I had reps turning us in to all kinds of three-letter agencies, posting bad reviews, stealing from us, and so on until I learned what I'll tell you.

When it's time for someone to leave an organization, it's usually the best thing for both parties. The person leaving has normally been stressed out for months and hasn't been contributing to the company; that's one of the worst feelings a human has to endure. Working where you're being looked down on and viewed as incompetent comes in a close second.

When you look at firing people, you're really looking to help them find a place where they would be better fits. It's not that they're bad people; it's that they're not being fully utilized at your company. Once managers understand that such people will be better off after they leave, they can start thinking about the best way to let them go.

Before I fire someone, I write down all the things he or she did well while at my organization. Depending on the person, I may even write him or her a letter of recommendation for another position that would be a good fit. If I had a woman in sales who was horrible, I might write that she had excellent customer service skills and could do well in such a position.

I'll acknowledge all the good employees I'm firing did for the organization, thank them for being assets to the team and for taking the risk to join our organization, and let them know I valued our time together personally. I will then make it quick and tell them the terms of their exit.

After that, I like to try to set up something in the future to make sure they know I care about them. One of the best things you can do for them is to offer to be a reference for certain of their qualities—perhaps for their work ethic and attitude. Showing you're willing to still be there for them goes a long way to making them feel you care about them, and it keeps them from wanting to go out of their way to hurt you or your organization. Good coaching and instilling high performance in your organization will make firing less necessary, but it will always be a key responsibility of a sales manager.

Follow this template.

1. Recognize the good things they did.
2. Show them you care about them personally.
3. Keep the termination as short as possible if you're giving reasons.
4. Let them know you would be a reference for the things they did well thus showing a desire for a continued relationship.

3.15 How to Handle an Employee Review

Employee reviews have become extinct in most sales cultures. I've even forgotten to write these reviews at times. In many sales organizations, raises are not an issue because commissions are the main driver of income. It almost feels worthless to do a review if you're not giving an employee a raise.

At their core, reviews are ways to recognize, acknowledge, and show appreciation for the growth of an employee. In sales, formal reviews might not be as important as informal reviews. During these reviews, the focus is on what great things reps have done since their last reviews—higher performance and better numbers for instance; that can be powerful and easy to understand.

In my organization, we have a goal for all of our reps—making $200k annually. We track where they are on that journey but more important how they're doing compared to the previous year. We analyze numbers that show growth so I can point out how they're getting better, not where they need improvement. Remember to always instill high-performance beliefs in your team. If your reps believe in their high-performance abilities, they'll find and fix their faults on their own. Pointing out their faults will put them on the defensive, while pointing out their strengths will make them grow, and that's what you want. Point out their gifts and blessing and watch their sales numbers improve exponentially.

Employee reviews should be done once a quarter; they should be quick and not even called reviews; I normally call them, "Got a second?" I want just to quickly build some performance in reps and get them to leave our meetings feeling elevated and ready to step into a higher level of performance. Making this process causal helps remove expectations and stress.

Most employees feel raises are tied to employee reviews. For instance, if there is no compensation change, it shouldn't be called a review. "Honey, I had a review today. It went great, but no raise. Yeah, I know. I really need to go work somewhere where they appreciate me." I know that may seem odd, but this happens all the time with new managers who don't understand what people expect with reviews. If you must call them reviews, make sure you frame them as quick meetings to address what your reps are doing great—not salary conversations, just meetings that address their strengths.

Keeping track of the reviews is key. Recapping previous reviews is another way to show growth and refocus. Reviews compared to previous reviews will provide the most benefit to reps. They will always question numbers, but if they can see and remember the first set of numbers from their last review and see their growth, they'll be more likely to make a shift in their beliefs about their performance. Your parents used to measure your height on a door frame, right? Any measurement would have been irrelevant if you couldn't compare it to previous measurements. Reviews can move your team members from one level to the next.

And never forget an employee's one-year, five-year, and ten-year anniversaries. Some of them started with hair and now have none. Show your appreciation for the years they've devoted to your organization.

3.16 How to Hire a Sales Rep

Hiring is the single biggest responsibility sales managers have. If you have a great team, you'll achieve your targets. If you have a team with a few bad apples, they can ruin morale and cause serious issues.

My manager Neil, whom I mentioned earlier, told me there were only two things that mattered when you hired someone—skill and will. If you find someone with both, hire that person. If you have a great training program, hire someone with will and then add the skill, but don't hire anyone with skill who lacks will. In a job interview, assess will; resumes will demonstrate the skills.

Here are the main components of will: Will they actually do the job? Will they do it long term? Will the job reinforce their nature? Let's say you have an applicant with bad back pain who worked for a moving company for forty years and won multiple awards. How would you access his will? I'd give him one point out of three. We know the job reinforces his nature since he's done it for forty years, but we're unsure if he can keep that up.

Someone else has been in sales for fifteen years and has won multiple awards. In the interview, you ask him where he sees himself in five years, and he says being a full-time preacher at his church. You give him one out of three on will. The above candidate can clearly handle the job, but it doesn't reinforce his nature and he has dated how long he will work with you. Interviewees are always more optimistic about how long they will work for a company than they really are. If they say they'd stay five years, they will leave; within a year or two tops, they'll be looking for something else. They may not be leaving, but when one foot's out the door, performance suffers.

Having good questions you consistently ask interviewees helps make sure you catch all the will issues early on before you hire and train someone. Some companies even make a person get on the phone and role-play just to make sure they really have the skill and want the job enough to push for it. Taking an hour with new candidates before you hire them is a very good idea. It can take three to six months to train an employee, so don't waste your time by making a bad hire. I normally bring people back two to three times before I offer a job just to make sure they're really committed to the position. By bringing them back more, they'll feel they actually got something special by being awarded the position.

After you've selected and want to offer a job to a new hire, make the candidate sell you on getting the job. Have you ever had anyone not show up the first day? I bet the hiring manager forgot this step. Don't suffer the same fate; pay attention.

I ask these questions.

1. Please rank this opportunity on a scale of one to ten. What would make it a ten?
2. What do you like most about our company?
3. Why do you want to work for our company?
4. If you're hired here, where do you see yourself in five years?
5. Why are you the best candidate to hire for the position?

The answers help make sure candidates are selling themselves on wanting to work for your company. My goal when I make a job offer is to get the hire excited and to feel fortunate to have beaten out the other candidates. Hiring is your single best return on the investment of your time. It's so much easier to sharpen a knife than it is to forge one from scratch. Hire wise and your job as a sales manager will be rewarding.

CONCLUSION

We've spent a lot of time together on this journey into the modern sales process. So much has been changed by the internet and social media. Consumers prefer to buy things online with the click of a button versus talking to a salesperson because they're still afraid of salespeople and being sold. Rather, consumers are looking for subject matter experts they can gain knowledge from quickly. Google has spoiled everyone; our patience for answers is nonexistent. To succeed in sales today, you have to learn what the buyer needs and deliver a unique solution quickly.

Even though today's consumers need everything super quick, they still crave relationships and connections—go figure. When you're selling your solution, it's important to make the presentation fun, exciting, and interactive to keep the prospects' precious attention. So many reps nowadays have canned presentations that don't allow for feedback from and interaction and involvement with clients. **We learned that questions are the best way to engage and maintain prospects.**

On this journey, we covered sales, marketing yourself, and managing a team. In the sales part, we learned the key components of a sales presentation and the fallout points where we lose momentum in the sales process. We identified the open, appointments, appointments that show up, conversations, proposals, and closes. We learned that if you do not set good appointments, you'll have a lot of no-shows. Getting a client to confirm and sending an email reminder is a great way to prevent missed appointments.

We learned about fair enough, a close that allows you to get the clients to quickly focus not on the best deal but on a fair deal. Fair deals are the only deals that close long term. We looked at the biggest reasons sales reps leave companies—losing interest in the product they're selling. We addressed how to prevent this from happening through success stories. We addressed why you need to master your CRM and understand the best ways this tool can make you money. We also addressed how to interview and find the right sales job.

In the next part of the book, we talked about how to promote yourself. We addressed how to speak on different stages and how to generate your own leads and be able to really set your own income. We addressed webinars and how positioning yourself as a subject matter expert will bring in leads and increase your closing rate. Clients want to interact with gurus, not salespeople. The internet has allowed anyone with a smartphone to develop a web presence that rivals those of even the biggest companies. We showed you how to simply make your web presence your new closing machine. We tied in all aspects of marketing from how to get referrals to how to work affiliates. In each of the sections in the marketing part of this book, we addressed the key ways to get leads and more important how to close a higher percentage of those leads. We learned that when a consumer sees a video or a webinar you have done, they'll be much more likely to buy from you.

Last, we talked about sales management and how even if you'll never be a sales manager, you still need to understand what your sales manager does so you can better manage yourself. We also always want to be offered such positions; we can always turn them down. We learned that a sales manager is a friend who coaches reps to operate at higher levels of performance. The manager sets the benchmarks for performance and makes sure each rep hits performance numbers. Sales managers build the confidence of their reps by appreciating and acknowledging their performance and using it to condition higher performance. **Great sales managers will be viewed as friends and mentors, not bosses. They lead their teams from a position of gratitude and love, not power and superiority.**

When I'm coaching leaders, I get them to write down the characteristics and traits of the best managers they had, and they turn out to be caring, loving, friendly, motivating, passionate, and understanding. How would your team describe you? What do you need to change to become the leader you want to be?

I acknowledge your growth in finishing this book. On average, CEOs read a book a week while average Americans are lucky to finish one book per year. My goal in writing this book was to have you want to finish it and then implement it what you have learned. Take five minutes to write down all the things you learned in this book that you'll implement. Do that now while it's fresh; that makes future recollection easier.

I also have included my implementation plan below as a bonus to you for finishing the book.

Implementation Guide—How to Get Started

After the first week, pick the parts of the implementation guide you want to repeat. Do this with your team at least once per quarter. And role-playing should never stop.

Pick a buddy at the office to do this with. Set a time daily and share your results with each other. Rerun this same list every day. Role-playing is so important that we do it every day. I want everyone's throat warmed up; we don't want to practice on customers.

Day 1—Role-Play

Create daily role-play content for remainder of week.

We role-play every day off the script and/or plan that comes out of this role.

What questions should you ask the client? Role-play these with your team. Get them burned deep in their brains so they become automatic.

Questions

What are the parts of my sales process?

What parts can I make more efficient?

What is the current script for this section? If I don't have one, how can I create one?

What are some really good questions I should memorize to ask clients?

Date 2—State Changes

What can I do to get my clients to snap out of unresourceful states quickly? Think about how you change when someone tells you something or does something. Can you have a quick joke to bring everyone back to full attention?

Practice taking a client that is complaining about price and getting him to focus on something else. This is called a pattern interrupt. Practice doing this with a partner.

Day 3—Rep Coaching

Sit next to a rep and listen or get an audio call sent to you.
What did the rep do great?
Did the rep recommend a large solution?
Did the rep pitch upsell?
What urgency did he use to get the deal in?
Ask the rep you coached what they do great on the call?

Day 4—Establishing Your Priorities

Set priorities for calling clients for renewals, new business, former clients, and upsells. Remember it's not just about new business.

This requires a holistic approach. Make sure your best clients are touched by a senior manager to make sure they are renewing with no issue.

Go over the previous week's numbers. How much revenue did you generate from each of the four segments? What segments do you need to focus on?

What were your big sales wins from the previous week?

Day 5—Conditioning Your Mind for Success

Write down the following every week.

1. How much have you made YTD? How much off are you from your next income target? Not knowing that is okay; just divide your YTD pretax earnings by how many weeks you've worked. This will give you an idea of your income per week.
2. Why is your solution the best value for your prospects?
3. What is the next step in income for you?
4. Why do you want to earn the next level of income? Is it for your family, you, the fact that others told you that you would never be this successful? What is it?
5. Only you know the plan that will work for you; let's put one together.

I bid you farewell and hope to meet you soon and connect with you online. Drop me a line at my LinkedIn contact below and let me know how this book impacted you. If you have any questions on the content, I'm available for clarification. I'd love to hear from you. In the meantime, I wish you success and happiness.

https://www.linkedin.com/in/dan-d-driscoll/

www.ingramcontent.com/pod-product-compliance
Lightning Source LLC
Chambersburg PA
CBHW021358210526
45463CB00001B/151